Twists and Turns
The Tommy Burns Story

To Rosemary, who was the making of Tommy Burns. I love you more each day.

* * *

To Our Blessed Lady. My thanks for carrying me through all the hard times and keeping my feet on the ground on the many great times.

Your servant.

* * *

To the Celtic Supporters. Thanks for accepting me. You'll never walk alone.

TOMMY BURNS

Twists and Turns

The Tommy Burns
Story

As told to
HUGH KEEVINS

Foreword by
ROY AITKEN

SPORTSPRINT PUBLISHING
EDINBURGH

Our thanks to D.C. Thomson Ltd
and to *The Celtic View*
for permission to reproduce pictures in this book.

© Tommy Burns and Hugh Keevins 1989

Reprinted 1989

ISBN 0 85976 286 6

Phototypeset by Beecee Typesetting Services
Printed in Great Britain by Bell & Bain Ltd., Glasgow

Foreword

Tommy Burns and myself go back a long way. We came into the Celtic team together at the same time, in 1975, and we started to make names for ourselves in 1977, the year the club won the Premier League and Scottish Cup double under the late Jock Stein. Our friendship was well and truly cemented, though, when the two of us visited Houston, Texas in 1978 to stay with Bobby Lennox, who has now come back to work at Celtic Park.

Celtic players tend, habitually, to have a respect for, and understanding of, each other because we know what it is like to live under the pressure that comes with being in one half of the Old Firm. The first thing I would like to say about Tommy Burns, therefore, is that I would have to compliment him for the way in which he has responded so impeccably to those demands. I would say that he has shown himself to be one of Celtic's greatest ever servants.

Tommy's kind of loyalty and devotion to Celtic is something that is rarely seen now in the modern-day game and has led to him developing a special relationship with our supporters, as vouched for when over forty thousand of them turned out to pay tribute to him on the occasion of his testimonial in 1987.

It has also been a pleasure to play beside such a talented performer who should have had his abilities recognised more often than they were at international level with Scotland. Everyone knows about that elegant left foot of his, and the right one isn't so bad, either, I can tell you! It is Tommy's general awareness and overall ability that have raised him above the normal and it has been our club's good fortune that he is a Celtic man through and through.

We have come through a lot together, Tommy and myself, so much so that it is pointless trying to isolate any one game to sum up the contribution he has made to Celtic, and if he has been outspoken on occasion on the park I know him to be a quiet, unassuming man away from the game and a fitting vice-captain beside me at Celtic Park.

I know, too, that his book will be like the man himself, honest, fair and full of class. It is my greatest wish that we have many more tremendous days together for Celtic.

Roy Aitken

Preface

Playing for Celtic's supporters has been a magical experience for me, the Thomas Burns who came from the Calton, ten minutes' walk from Paradise, and who grew up during the club's most magical era. I have had a career to date which has given me six League Championship, five Scottish Cup and one League Cup winners medal as well as eight caps for Scotland. However, my greatest achievement, in my opinion, has been to survive for so long as a creative player with Celtic, since there have been very few Celts who last into their thirties after having started their careers at Celtic Park.

Having read many football books about the lives of great players, I have found a certain formula about them all. When I was approached to write my own, therefore, I found I didn't want to go on about my favourite players or best eleven, etc. I wanted to put down my own thoughts, hopes, dreams, ambitions and frustrations, as experienced throughout my career with Celtic and their lovely supporters, who have been the greatest thing about the club in my time there.

In this book you will find no funny stories, and not because there haven't been any. It is because I have always taken the game too seriously and prefer to write about how I have felt at different stages of my career, both as a player and as a person rather than fill the pages with old football gags. You will find no tales of birds and booze in hotels on trips abroad, just the story of Thomas Burns from Soho Street who wanted nothing more out of life than to play for the 'Tic.

Many things in this book are of a personal nature but as I

am writing it for supporters to read I prefer not to kid them on but to write my story as I have lived it, good, bad, up and down. In opening up my heart I may not turn out to be the most popular guy in certain quarters but this is how it has been for Thomas Burns and I hope people appreciate it for what it is, simply my story, my opinion.

Thomas Burns

Contents

CHAPTER ONE

East Side Story

The parish of St. Mary's in the East End of Glasgow was the birthplace of Celtic Football Club and the focal point of the community into which I was born and brought up within walking distance of the ground where I have played since I was a boy of fifteen years old. I joined the club straight from the classroom, having first been a pupil at St. Mary's primary school, where I was educated by the Marist brothers, the religious order from which Brother Walfrid, Celtic's founder, came in the last century. My teacher was Brother Jerome, who would fill his pupils with the spirit of Celtic as well as the more conventional forms of know-

On the ball at an early age. One from the family scrapbook as I show my young cousin, Douglas Drummond, the rudiments of the game in Glasgow Green.

ledge and first noticed what potential I had for making my way in the game of football. There is, therefore, an emotional as well as an historical bond between the people of the East End and the institution that is Celtic and if I am, in some small way, a personification of that, then I can only say it has been my immense honour and privilege. Celtic never meant a means of making money to me and the best way that I can emphasise that briefly is by saying that if I had been given the choice of playing for any other club and winning one hundred caps for Scotland it could not possibly have been better than simply being known as Tommy Burns of Celtic and winning the medals I have done with them.

To the working class citizens of Glasgow, football is a weekly release from the ordinariness of their own lives. Their team is a cause with which they can identify and also take pride in while sometimes struggling along, and being let down, in other ways. The modern day, re-emerging Glasgow city centre is a place to which those from the outlying areas come to stare at the splendour, able to look but not touch. For those who are that way inclined, Celtic Park on a Saturday represents a shared experience as well as colour and excitement. I like to think I can associate with the Celtic supporters who come from a background identical to my own, and within the pages of this book it is my intention to try and convey what our club has meant to me over the years and what the affection and devotion of the people who follow the team has given to the players like myself at the same time.

Playing football professionally was not a means of escape from anything else where I was concerned. Instead, it would be more accurate to say that being a Celtic player was all I ever wanted out of life for myself. I am not ashamed or embarrassed to say that I would would pray every night as a youngster for the chance to join the club that felt like a part of my very being. At one time, I felt I would have gladly given my life for the opportunity to wear a hooped jersey and if maturity, and the importance of my wife, Rosemary, and my children, Emma, Jenna and Michael, has given me a different perspective, it has not diminished in any way my regard for the club, the nobility of its origins or the place it holds in people's lives.

Celtic were brought into being to look after the welfare of the needy children who were born into the streets like the one I lived in, at no. 43 Soho Street in that district of Glasgow known by no other geographical definition than the Calton. If poverty on the tragic scale of the nineteenth century was no longer evident in 1956, the living was still far from easy when I became the middle child of Thomas and Margaret Burns the week before Christmas. With my two sisters, Elizabeth, the oldest of the family, and Anne, I stayed in a post-war block of flats which stood beside the more decayed tenements in a street that then had as its main claim to fame the fact that Marie Lawrie had once been a resident there. Marie went on to change her name and become known to audiences everywhere as Lulu. The rest of us did our singing at Celtic Park and tried to make our way in the world as best we could.

Scholastically speaking, Tommy Burns was not going to be an academic, something which Brother Jerome had deduced very early on along with my more natural inclination towards kicking a ball. When the time came to move on to secondary school, in fact, it was the priest who took me aside and pointed out the alternatives. On the one hand there was St. Mungo's, one of Glasgow's more notable Catholic schools with a proud record of turning out the educationally accomplished. If I decided to go there, this, Brother Jerome told me, would involve plenty of homework and an emphasis on study. We then arrived at the mutual understanding that this was not a lifestyle in keeping with my nature.

St. Mary's Secondary, he advised me, would pay dutiful attention to the educational basics on my behalf as well as offer me the opportunity to progress with the first organised team I played for, the local Boys' Guild side attached to the church. There was no longer any need for prolonged debate on the subject.

In the course of any player's career there are influential people who have to be thanked for making valuable contributions in one way or another. In my case, Brother Jerome was one such person but a man called John Rice had an even more profound effect on me and helped shape the way I eventually turned out. Harmful temptations outside of the home were plentiful in the Calton and, regrettably, accounted for more than one promising boy player who might have gone on to achieve anything that I have, and possibly more, had they been able to be resisted. This is not by any stretch of the imagination to look down on those who fell by the wayside. There but for the grace of God, and John Rice, go I. The Boys' Guild was a way of taking people like myself off the streets we used to roam at nights. Suitable diversion was hard to come by and myself and my pals would find ours, innocently enough, by hanging around until the pubs came out at eleven o'clock and then watching the best of the impromptu boxing contests that would go on among the men inflamed by the drink they had just taken. John Rice would try to channel our energies into more positive areas, insisting that we train under his supervision every night and then go straight home without waiting for the pavement cabaret artistes.

I would look up to the older ones I met at the Boys' Guild and adopt them as my first heroes for the way they could play football. If some of them paid no heed to John's words about the virtues of keeping to the straight and narrow, I would also have to acknowledge that there were also those who would take an interest in the promising teenagers and encourage them in their progress, even if that meant only turning them away from the pub doorway they were about to enter themselves. The nearest I got to intoxication was drooling over the ability of friends of mine like Tam McGarvey, Gerry MacNamara, Hughie Farrell and Eddie 'Pie' Semple.

Years later, I remember Kenny Dalglish, when he was still with Celtic, telling me about one boy in particular

A motley looking crew, but a successful team. Eastercraigs under 16 side and I'm the one with the neat hair third from the right in the front row.

from St. Mary's who had been brought to train at Celtic Park and was an immediate revelation using the talent that had been nurtured, like so many before him, in the back streets of Glasgow. Kenny couldn't understand what had happened to him because he disappeared from sight as quickly as he had arrived in their midst. I could have told Kenny, but didn't, that this friend of mine had gone to Blackpool one Bank Holiday, become involved in a fight and ended up in jail. It is also only fair to point out that he has since done well for himself and is a successful businessman. This was during that period when Glasgow was becoming notorious for its gang warfare. To live in the Calton, for example, was to be associated with, whether or not you belonged to, the Calton Tongs or the San Toi and this led to me having to learn the hard way about sticking up for myself. My decision to attend St. Mary's Secondary school had been taken when the building was still situated, for want of a better description, on our patch, though I would have to make it clear that I never ran with a gang in my life. By the time I was due to go there, however, St.

Mary's had been moved to different premises in the nearby Barrowfield area. This was only a short distance away but it was, more importantly, the preserve of two other gangs, the Torch and the Spur. For those who don't know about these things, the names and the territorial mentality make all this sound like Cagney's immortal 'Angels With Dirty Faces' or the romanticised street life of 'West Side Story', but I can assure you there was no snappy dialogue or choreographed dancing in the East End production!

My homework in the evenings consisted of drawing diagrams outlining how best to get to and from school in one piece and while still wearing what I had come out with that morning. No-one went to St. Mary's wearing a school uniform or anything that was remotely new or fashionable because to do so was to provoke trouble, and there was already enough of that without sending out invitations.

My most vivid recollections are of the razor gangs who would stalk the playground, either ripping some poor unfortunate's clothes to shreds or taking them from somebody else in a menacing way that put any idea of resistance out of the head altogether. This went on inside or outside the school building, and I can well recall the case of the two pupils who ignored all of the warnings and sneaked out one day to buy cigarettes. By the time they returned to the classroom, the pair of them were wearing only their underclothing, having been relieved of their expensive attire somewhere between the tobacconist's and the school. Needless to say, they had no cigarettes either.

The lengths I had to go to in order to get home safely were sometimes extraordinary, too, because of my own vanity. I had worn spectacles from the age of nine but never took them outside the house, which meant that anyone who decided to pick on me usually had their hands starting to squeeze my throat before I had even noticed they were there. Consequently, I would take this ridiculously roundabout way home, going to a nearby bus stop and then getting off the bus in a 'no-go' area before walking the rest of the way back to Soho Street. Even at that there was a time when I was waylaid by three of the local villains who wanted to take the duffle coat I was wearing. Contrary to what anyone who knows me might think, I do possess a fierce temper but it requires the first blow to be struck against me before the red mist descends. That night, one of my would-be assailants triggered off the explosion and I was still hitting him when his two accomplices were busily running down the road in the opposite direction. That story isn't something I'm proud of at all; in fact I was gripped by remorse afterwards even though I was only defending myself, and I only tell it because it offers an example of what it took at times to survive in the part of Glasgow where I struggled to grow up to a ripe old age. My careers officer at St. Mary's told me that I was an average pupil and could have stayed on to sit my 'O' levels and Highers. I told him that going there for as long as I had done had taken its toll of my nervous system and that I wanted out in case I didn't live long enough to get my leaving certificate.

As well as acts of violence, petty crime was another recurring theme of life among my peers, and to this day I still read on occasion about people I had gone to school with who have, unfortunately, gone to prison after graduating to more serious forms of theft, like armed robbery. Before John Rice's words about avoiding street corners had fully permeated my brain, I did witness a couple of incidents which hardly ranked with the Great Train Robbery but were sufficiently nerve-wracking to banish for good the idea of dallying on the way home. On one occasion I was actually asked to keep a look-out for the police, even though I was so short-sighted I would have missed the entire Serious Crime Squad if they had arrived on the pavement. Fear can do wonderful things for the myopic, though, and I did manage to spot two of Glasgow's finest from a way off while a couple of acquaintances of mine were investigating the inside of a van that was to deliver chocolate bars. The feeling of terror I experienced raising the alarm and then making off into the night, even though I was a completely innocent party, never left me. The experience guaranteed that, whatever else my family had to worry about, they need never fear for their son embarking on a life of crime.

I stayed out of trouble because of John Rice and the haven that his Boys' Guild offered me and also because I could never have contemplated doing anything that would have made my mother ashamed of me. My father worked away from home for most of the time and my parents separated when I was fifteen, though they have always remained on civilised terms, but through it all my mother would never allow slackness of any kind among her children. My sisters and myself were the products of what is known as a mixed marriage in that my father was a Catholic and my mother a Protestant. Every Sunday morning, though, it was my mother who made sure that we attended to our religious duties and got us up in time to go to mass.

My mother couldn't take us herself but she would find out what time the family downstairs were going and we would go off to St. Mary's with the Collins's. One of them, Gerry, now plays for Patrick Thistle and has remained my closest friend as well as being one of Celtic's staunchest supporters. Because of my upbringing in respect of my mother looking after the family's religious obligations, I have no time for bigotry. If everyone now knows me to be devoted to Celtic and what the club stands for, that doesn't mean I deny anyone else the right to feel the same way about Rangers. They're perfectly entitled to be right behind their team, and if a Rangers supporter stops me in the street, and some do, to talk about what is going on within the game I like to think there is mutual respect and understanding.

My mother didn't want me to become a Celtic player because she wanted no part of sectarian division, either, and when I was younger I would try to please her by saying that I would join Manchester United when I grew up. The older I became, though, the first thing I knew I had to do if I

Wee Tommy from the Calton during the days when I was laundry boy to the famous at Celtic Park.

was to sign for anyone was distance myself from what was happening around me and start to live like an athlete. My sisters used to ask me if I thought it was worth it to deny myself the pleasures enjoyed by the other boys my age in order to try and attain my hopes and dreams and I could always truthfully answer them that it was if I could join Celtic. That's why I feel a certain sense of responsibility now to the young players I meet at Celtic Park, passing on any advice I think might be helpful, and why there is one date that is permanently marked in my diary every year. That is when I go back to present the prizes to the boys of St. Mary's Boys' Guild football team at the annual ceremony that is still presided over by John Rice. For me, he epitomises all that's good about the East End of Glasgow, and but for him I wouldn't have started on the road that led to Celtic Park, even if that short journey involved taking a sizeable detour through Middlesbrough.

Even when I was only eleven years old, John arrived for

me in his car one day and said he was taking me to Celtic Park. He did, too, all the way to the front door, where he rang the bell and asked to see Sean Fallon, who was then assistant manager. Sean was out at the time but Jim Kennedy, who works in the club's offices and was a Celtic player himself at one time, was there. John told him that I should be signed by Celtic. Just like that, at the age of eleven! As I recall, Jim peered down from the enquiry window and looked at me as if I had landed from outer space. It was the kind of blank stare he gives me now when I ask for extra tickets for big matches, so you can understand the debt of gratitude I feel I owe to John Rice. At the time, I was probably more impressed by getting a 'hurl' in his car, but I'll never forget the kindness of the man who had so much faith in me and was also the person who gave me my first pair of football boots.

Middlesbrough, though, were the first senior club to show an interest in me after I had survived one last complication involving the Glasgow gangland scene. I had been invited to take part in a trial for the Glasgow schoolboys' under-15 side. The training session, though, was being held in Easterhouse, which had become the high profile centre of the media's attention to the problem after the visit made there by the entertainer, Frankie Vaughan. Frankie's missionary work in the sixties had obviously not led to the total conversion of all the teenage residents of that housing scheme, because my first visit there was also my last. Incredible as it may sound, I couldn't go back to press for a place in the team because I was chased out of Easterhouse that night for no other reason than that I came from a different part of the city, and there was no inclination to try for a second opinion.

By this time, a week in Middlesbrough was beginning to sound like a holiday on the Riviera. I went down in the company of two other boys from Glasgow, Ian Kennedy and Jim Scotland, and by the end of that time I felt I had done enough to be offered a more permanent arrangement at Ayresome Park. The manager of the club then was a nice man called Stan Anderson, who patiently told me that my progress with the Boys' Guild would be monitored and that I would be invited back during the next school holidays. In spite of the fact that Ian and Jim were told the same thing, the news couldn't have sounded any worse to me if they had been playing the funeral march in the background. I telephoned my mother from the railway station before starting the journey home to Glasgow and it was all I could do to stop myself from crying as I told her what had happened. I thought it was the end of the world, but on the way back something my two travelling companions had said to me came into my mind. Ian and Jim had gone to Middlesbrough as only the first of a series of clubs to be visited, a common practice among the boys from the team they played with, Eastercraigs. It was then I decided to ask them for a game and leave the Boys' Guild for a better class of competition and the regular opportunity of being seen by scouts from the bigger senior clubs.

Being brought up in the East End had taught me to have an opinion of my own and stick to it, so, while I felt bad about leaving St. Mary's, I knew instinctively that I was doing the right thing. It didn't take long, either, for my initiative to produce the best result of all because, two months after I started to play in the respected Scottish Amateur League, a representative from Celtic asked me if I would like to start training once a week at Celtic Park.

Anyone then who had red hair and was on the small side was instantly compared to Jimmy Johnstone. There was even the time when I was carried out of the Celtic end of our ground on the shoulders of an excitable crowd because I had his colouring and build. Jimmy had scored the winning goal in the last minute of a game against Dundee United, and since an invasion of the pitch to honour the real thing was out of the question I became a substitute for the wee man. My style of play was nothing like his, though, but it was sufficiently impressive for Willie Fernie, another tremendous former Celtic player, who was looking after the club's youngsters in the early seventies.

Willie was the first man at Celtic Park to speak to Sean Fallon about me after what had been an inauspicious start to my time there. I've been told that when the late Mr Stein first set eyes on the skinny, insignificant-looking kid from down the road his initial reaction was, 'Who has made a mistake and sent us him?' I didn't help myself, either, when it came time for us to exchange our first words. I was sitting in one of the dressing rooms with two boys of my own age, Rab Prentice, who later went on to play for Hearts and Dundee, and Jimmy Kyles, who came from Tayside. The manager, who had taken a sympathetic interest in my welfare by that stage, put his head round the door and asked me if I was settling down OK.

There's another characteristic of people from places like the Calton, and that's a total absence of any self-consciousness. Regardless of the fact that he was the legendary Jock Stein, idolised, even canonised, by the Celtic supporters for what he had done to transform an ordinary team into European Cup winners and unarguably the finest side in the modern-day history of Scottish football, he was, to a boy from Soho Street, nothing except big Jock. But when I answered his question by saying, 'Aye, fine, Jock,' I thought the other two were going to choke because they were trying so hard to suppress their laughter. None of this helped me relax inside the place because, subconsciously, I had felt all along that I had no right to be at Celtic Park at the same time as the players like Jimmy Johnstone, Bobby Lennox and Billy McNeill I was still cheering from the terracing every chance I got.

It was Willie Fernie who helped calm me down with words of praise and also an unusual request. He had been going to Jock Stein after I had left every Tuesday night and telling him that I was running all over the pitch, putting the ball through the other players' legs and generally doing enough to merit a signing offer. While he worked on wearing down the big man, Willie told me that I could provide the conclusive touch in the negotiations for myself by getting a severe haircut. Like every other teenager in

One of the immortal 'Lisbon Lions', Stevie Chalmers, presents me with a magazine award.

1971, I had shoulder-length hair but it was shorn the day after Willie told me that might make a difference. Shortly before Christmas that year, as I was being dropped off after training with Eastercraigs, Ian Stevenson, who was our coach, told me that Celtic had asked to sign me. The prayers had been answered.

Now, eighteen years on, I drive past St. Mary's, what remains of Soho Street and then my old school every morning on the way to Celtic Park and it's hard not to be reminded of all that went into achieving my lifetime's ambition.

We're all to some extent a product of our environment and the Calton gave me an attitude to life for which I'm grateful. I wouldn't change a single thing about the way I was brought up, and to this day I still feel more at home talking to old friends from the East End than I do sitting in one of Glasgow's more splendid hotels wearing a dinner suit and a bow tie. It isn't that I feel inferior to the people I'm mingling with on these formal occasions, more that I believe I will find a deeper level of sincerity in the Calton. The Celtic supporters will know what I'm talking about and they more than repaid me for anything I might have done for them by the genuine warmth of their response when 42,000 of them turned out for my testimonial game against Liverpool in 1987. Like the people of the Calton for me, they're always there when Celtic need them.

The later I get in my career with the club, the more deeply I cherish every game I play in the green and white hoops, too. And when it's all over for me as a player, something I want to do one day is take my son, Michael, walking along London Road wearing his Celtic scarf, just as I see all the other fathers doing with their children at present. When Michael is old enough to ask me how it all started for his dad at Celtic Park, though, the first thing I will have to tell him is that when I arrived at the moment I had hoped and prayed for I suddenly changed my mind and said I wasn't signing for the club!

CHAPTER TWO

He And I

It is better sometimes to journey, as the saying goes, than it is to arrive. My longing to become a Celtic player ought to have been over, and the job of fulfilling my ambition begun, on the night that I went to Celtic Park with my dad and my guiding light, John Rice, to sign the form that would tie me to the club as a schoolboy. Instead, I was suddenly engulfed by a feeling of insecurity, and the enormity of what I was on the verge of doing made me have second thoughts. John Higgins, who was then Celtic's chief scout, listened patiently while I explained that Everton and Leeds United both wanted me to go on trial with them and that my idea was to see what happened in England first before coming back to talk over my future with Celtic. Subconsciously, I think I had walked into the ground that night and allowed the previous six years of the club's undiluted success so far as the domestic scene was concerned to wash all over me, temporarily drowning my confidence as it did so. When what should have been the greatest moment in my life arrived, I actually heard myself saying 'no' to Celtic.

John Higgins had pointed out that the Club was not really entitled to wait on me coming back from England and take a chance on a change of mind. They were offering me the opportunity to sign straight away. I could tell that my two elders were disappointed when I left the room without signing and I could sense that I really didn't know my own mind at the time. Joining Celtic was the dream of most boys in the Calton, but was it ever supposed to come true? The intrusion of reality had left me confused. It was then that fate lent a hand to clear up the problem. As we walked down the corridor, passing the board room on one side, the shamrock-shaped memorial to one of the club's legendary players, John Thomson, on the other, John Higgins very generously offered to show us Celtic's trophy room, the holy of holies so far as any committed supporter of the team is concerned. As the wee boy from the East End stood transfixed, looking at the Scottish Cup, the replica of the European Cup that had been given to Celtic after their historic achievement in Lisbon and the League Championship trophy, which seemed to have been taken into permanent custody at Celtic Park, the imaginary crowd noises that filled my head along with instantly recalled visions of crucial goals that had been scored were interrupted by a voice echoing in my ear. 'Do you really know what you're doing, Thomas? This is Celtic you're turning down, after all.'

It was my dad, who had never in his life interfered with anything I had wanted to do but, on this occasion, could foresee an immense mistake being about to be made. It was precisely the jolt to the nervous system that I needed and, after a quick, confirmatory discussion with John Rice, I went up to John Higgins and asked if it would be all right to change my mind and borrow his pen after all. If opening the door to the trophy room had been a piece of improvised coercion, then it had worked beautifully. The funny thing was that after I had signed the form and stood outside 95 Kerrydale Street for the first time as a Celtic player the former quivering wreck felt a changed person. By the time I had walked home and told my mother, I knew I had never felt happier or more contented. In fact, when people ask me now if, after so many years with the same team, I ever get bored and yearn for a change, I think back to that night and the answer is always the same. Restless-ness might have been a problem had the club in question been any other apart from Celtic but my passion for them has been an eternal flame inside me that has never needed to be rekindled by anything. I have been fortunate enough to have been sustained throughout my entire career by two

Off and running — closely marked by the referee.

things: one is my devotion to Celtic and the feelings they inspire in people and the other is my belief in God.

There would be no point to this book at all if the reader got to the end without having gained any insight into me as a human being as well as a professional football player, and the truth is that I see my religious beliefs as going hand in hand with my career. There is equally no doubt that one day my time will be up and retirement from the limelight will follow. I will still have a life to lead as any other normal person, though, and I would want to conduct that life in as decent a way as possible. It does not embarrass me to discuss my faith in public because I'm not doing so to impress anyone or to have people think of me as what would be called a goody-goody. I turn to God at every opportunity because I am no different from anybody else and because I accept that I am sufficiently frail to need His help and guidance more than most.

As the story of how I eventually came to sign for Celtic illustrates, I'm frequently unsure of myself. There hasn't been any one person in particular throughout my life that I have felt so close to I could go to him, or her, and discuss my innermost doubts, fears or hopes. When I want to do that I talk to God and ask Him to get me through every day of my life. I try, as a practising Catholic, to go to mass and take Holy Communion every morning before I go to Celtic Park. There was also a time when I would go into the church on my own later on in the day just to sit there for ten minutes and ask for God's help. If anyone who knew me as a Celtic player happened to see me coming out, I would become self-conscious but gradually it dawned on me that I had absolutely nothing to feel uneasy about.

It doesn't bother me, either, that other players might not respect my views on God. All I know is that I couldn't have stayed in top-class football at club level for as long as I have done had I not been fortified by the sacraments of the church. I don't get down on my knees and ask God to make Celtic win or force the opposition to do badly, all I ask is the strength to play my part and then I will do all in my earthly power to use the talent I have been given. There is no difficulty, either, in equating my religious obedience with the life of a professional footballer, which some people may perceive as a selfish preoccupation with contracts, money and self-advancement and, therefore, hardly in keeping with the Commandments. I have always asked my employers, Celtic, for what I considered to be the fairest rate for the job I was doing, nothing more, nothing less, which makes me the same as every other working man in the country, I would imagine. At the same time I'm aware of my own spirituality and also humbled by the effect I can have as an individual on the lives of people who have never met me before just because I play for Celtic. I was written to once by a family who asked me to visit their elderly father in Glasgow's Western Infirmary, where he was trying to come to the end of his life, as a result of cancer, with as much dignity as was possible.

The two tumours in his brain and the medication this man was taking made his eyesight poor, his speech slow and his reactions dull, yet when I sat by his bedside and told him who I was there came an instant flicker of recognition and an anxiety to say something back to me. Moments like that, and my implicit belief in God, have given me a sense of perspective and kept the daily demands of football at a tolerable level.

It was with God's help that I was able to make it through the early, occasionally demoralising years at Celtic Park. I thought I could make it there as a player but it took a lot to convince some others. From being a schoolboy signing, who was given five pounds a week in expenses, I was taken on to the ground staff by Sean Fallon in 1972 at double the money, or, as Sean put it, 'Some extra for your mother'. Playing for Celtic Boys' Club at that age was practically compulsory in the eyes of Jock Stein but, once again, my habitual insecurity took over and that led to me learning the first, essential lesson about what it takes to become a Celtic player.

The Boys' Club is run by a man called Frank Cairney, who rarely gets the credit he deserves but will be recognised here for his efforts because, but for him, there might not have been a Tommy Burns at Celtic Park. To wear a green and white hooped jersey for the first time in an organised capacity was to be made aware of the fact that there are people for whom the jersey in itself is a source of provocation. I can remember visiting little pockets of hostility throughout the country where the level of abuse was remarkable, so much so I decided after only three months that I had to get away from all the ill-feeling and go back to playing for Eastercraigs. I even got to the stage of telephoning my old coach, Ian Stevenson, and arranging to meet him in the centre of Glasgow to talk over my difficulties. Older heads should always be consulted because, as I found out, the benefit of experience is invaluable to a mixed-up youngster.

With the assistance of hindsight, I can see now that what I was really after was the easy option, but it is not possible to be a Celtic player without the accompanying pressure, even if that is only people on the touchline making offensive remarks about your religious persuasion. Ian Stevenson could see what was wrong because the first thing he pointed out was that, if I came back, more would be expected of me since I was a year older. Frank Cairney's psychology was to hint that several boys had failed to make it with Celtic as a consequence of having gone from the protective sight of the Boys' Club, from where reports of every individual's progress would be relayed to the ultimate authority over who would, or would not, be signed on a full-time contract, Jock Stein. It may have been kidology but Frank Cairney also taught me more in a twelve-month period, once I had agreed to stay, than I would learn in many of the years that were to follow. The pressure that comes with expectation is something any Celtic player has to live with and developing good habits is another prerequisite for longevity in your playing career. That phrase may be baffling to the uninitiated but I have always taken it to mean helping others for the good of the team as a whole. Whatever happens, you can not hide so that you escape blame if things are not going well.

That is why if the crowd ever get upset with me now because I have made poor use of the ball I can handle it for

Celebrating, broken wrist and all, after Celtic's under 16 team had beaten Dundee to win the Scottish Cup and the referee failed to notice my 'stookie'.

the reason that I know I have at least accepted the ball from somebody else to help them out of a spot. Appreciating the value of teamwork meant so much to me by the end of my time with Celtic Boys' Club that I can remember winning the Scottish Cup for under sixteen year olds, against Dundee, while wearing a plaster cast on a broken wrist that went from my hand up to the elbow. The referee thought it was heavy bandaging and hadn't taken a close enough look, while a combination of being desperate to play and knowing that the team wanted me there convinced me I should take a personal risk. My physical development was going on at a remarkable rate all the while. In the time between signing my schoolboy form and joining Celtic on a full-time basis, I grew eight inches in height and filled out accordingly elsewhere. When it came time for me to make the next step up from the Boys' Club and go to a junior side, however, Jock Stein said 'no' to the one he still called 'wee Tommy'.

It was then that the stubbornness which came with an address in the Calton came to the fore once again and I made sure I not only went junior but picked a side who were in the lowest division in the West of Scotland and where I knew I would have to look after myself. I went to Maryhill Juniors because my neighbour and friend, Gerry Collins, played for them, and although I say so myself the team did exceptionally well. Big Jock, who was not used to having his better judgement questioned in that way, could do nothing about it by then but he eventually warmed to the idea and even turned up to watch us play at Pumpherston in a Scottish Junior Cup tie. Maryhill lost that day by the only goal of the game but I was told afterwards that Jock had said how pleased he had been with my unselfish running which meant that the fruits of Frank Cairney's labours were beginning to be seen. Besides which, while those around me on the ground staff at Celtic Park were former Scottish schoolboy caps, or had been asked to go with the Scotland Youth side, I had attained none of those distinctions and I had to make myself noticed.

Jock Stein had a beautiful smile and a vicious tongue, a tremendous sense of humour and a ferocious temper when he was roused. He could induce extreme apprehension in me one minute and then cause me to experience the greatest upsurge in confidence it was possible to get the next. Under his control, Celtic were still a force to be reckoned with in Europe when I was still at the stage of cleaning out the dressing rooms for the household names. Those big European nights were always savoured by the supporters and particularly those in a privileged position like myself. The groundstaff boys would be told to stay behind in the afternoon when the team was at home in Europe to perform all of the expected functions, like polishing the first team's boots and generally tidying up. There was always a point in the day, though, when I would sneak out on to the pitch just as the sun was going down and I had made sure the groundsman had put up the nets at each goal. In the fading light, and being glad of the silence inside the deserted ground, I would throw a ball up into the air so that I could volley it into the net and hear the rasp as the two met. It was a dream sequence that was usually interrupted by an irate groundsman threatening to tell the manager, but it was always worth the row.

Those moments of fantasy apart, it was a serious business for me under Jock Stein. Our first fall out, and my introduction to the hard side of making your way in the game, came one night before the reserve side left Celtic Park to play against Hamilton Accies. I sauntered into the ground not expecting to be playing at all. The second team, due to the overwhelming success of the first, was filled with people who were either no longer regulars in the first team or others who were simply not good enough to play at the highest level with Celtic. It was a criminal waste of young talent because it meant that a promising boy often found himself not getting a game for weeks on end and, therefore, had no opportunity to show what improvement he was making or, conversely, was unable to get anywhere because of insufficient match practice. Anyway, because I had walked in without a coat, the manager took that as a sign that I had assumed I would be playing and not sitting in a draughty stand all night, and jumping to conclusions like that was a dangerous form of exercise for players to take in front of him. Nothing, though, could have been further from the truth. The fact of the matter was that I had never got round to buying myself a coat. By then, I was earning twenty-seven pounds a week, had worn the same brown suit for a couple of years and was going out with a girl called Rosemary Smith as well as handing in money to my mother. There wasn't a lot left after that to make me a slave to fashion or even the climate.

Jock, though, called for Sean, asked to see the reserve team sheet and scribbled something on it while I looked on. To this day, I am convinced he was putting my name on the list and not taking it off, which is what I am sure he wanted me to think he was doing so that my bus journey to Lanarkshire would be spent contemplating the error of my ways and making resolutions never to take anything for granted and to remember always to wrap up well for night games. In any case, I played from the start at Douglas Park and felt confident enough to try out a couple of adventurous moves early on, neither of which came off. It was then I heard the bellowing noise coming from the stand. By the time I got near enough to the touchline to enable even my eyesight to let me see my critic, big Jock was there with smoke coming out of his ears, telling me that I had five minutes in which to do something correctly or I would be taken off. At least I think he said taken!

By half-time, I was still on the park but the manager saw to it that I never made it past the interval, telling me that I had played like an old man. That game, however, was one of half a dozen that I was given in quick succession, for which I thank God, because, but for them, the same fate might have befallen me as it did a large number of others who were released by Celtic at the end of that particular season. The casualty rate would not be so high today because the club now runs three teams in effect, one in the Premier Division, another in the Reserve League and one that takes part in what is known as the Reserve League West. So a large complement of players are able to get a regular game and a sporting chance to prove they can make the grade. The waste in the early seventies was not only confined to those who were freed being lost to Celtic, they were also taken away from the game at the highest level as the sense of devastation affected their lives on a deeply personal basis.

I knew that I was safe the day Jock came into the treatment room at Celtic Park and said to me, 'Remember, you're not far off the first team now, sir. Keep working hard.' It was just after I had played in a reserve game against Clydebank at Kilbowie Park. It was a tremendous

Five happy ground staff boys with Billy McNeill in 1972. Only one of us was still there in 1973, and I was that lucky person.
Left to right: Eddie Cattenach, Myself, Billy McNeill, Derek Barron, Mick Kelly and John Mulholland.

game with one youngster on the other side scoring a hat-trick and making sure Celtic had to work hard to win 6-5 in the end. His name was Davie Cooper. That game had shown Jock I had what it took to become a Celtic player. For him, that meant more than having a good game every now and then. It took the same high degree of commitment week in, week out and year in, year out. I had been fortunate enough to demonstrate what he was looking for when the reserves beat Partick Thistle and then St. Johnstone but, most of all, after we had won 2-0 against what was the entire Hibs first team, with the exception of Pat Stanton. They were being punished for having a bad result in the league but ended up making life even more difficult for themselves, even if they ensured it would be all the sweeter for me.

It was after that game I knew for sure within myself I could play at the very top. If I hadn't made it with Celtic, I had already been around the place long enough to know I would have been unable to take rejection by them. I don't know what I would have done with myself other than go home and lock myself indoors for six months to get over the embarrassment.

My most poignant memory of that time, though, is the night the rest of my friends were told they would not be getting kept on. It happened after a reserve match in which some of them had worn the hoops, unwittingly, for the last time. I sat in the foyer as, one by one, they came out of the manager's office with their eyes filling up with tears. When some people are given very bad news, they have a nervous, reflexive action that makes them want to laugh. That was how I felt, though I knew it was anything but a laughing matter. Since the memory is still so vivid in my mind, in fact, I will record, with respect, the names of whose who were freed and let them know that, even now, I think about them and still realise how lucky I was not to suffer that blow. There was John Mulholland . . . Davie Thomson . . . Jimmy Murphy . . . Gerry McAleer . . . Bernie Little . . . Colin Schaefer . . . Mick Kelly . . . Eddie Cattenach . . . Derek Barron . . . and Jim O'Donnell.

When I left the ground that night I thanked God for my career remaining intact and vowed that, with His help, I would work even harder to make it with Celtic. The important thing when you're a young player is not to have people tell you when you're playing badly. That much you can usually work out for yourself. The greatest help of all is to have someone there who can tell you exactly where you're going wrong. Perhaps there was a preoccupation with the first team at Celtic Park at that time, forcing the rest to fend for themselves. If I ever get the chance to run a side for myself, I will make sure I'm on hand whenever any of the younger players need assistance.

I will try to be someone like Frank Connor. When he was at Celtic Park in charge of the reserve side Frank practically lived with his players, and would have done if any of them had asked! He treated their development as the most important work of his life because he lived and breathed Celtic, and there are players around today, like Charlie Nicholas, who would gladly testify to that. So far as my upbringing at Celtic Park was concerned, it was once said to me by Frank Cairney that I had survived in spite, rather than because, of the system.

The concluding stage of my development from schoolboy to first-team player, though, was a very long way from Glasgow. If man ever sets up a colony on the moon, he may find that there are already a bunch of expatriate Scots there who are Celtic supporters. In 1975 there was a man in Rhodesia called Danny Murphy who ran a side called the Salisbury Callies and he wrote to Celtic asking if they would send out a player to guest with them for the summer time. Bobby Lennox was asked to go but had to refuse due to commitments with his young family. Brian McLaughlin was also unable to oblige as he was recovering from injury. Eventually, I agreed to go providing I had company and, insecure as ever, after my mother and my auntie had told me I would be mad to turn down an opportunity like that to see something of the world. That was how myself and another reserve, Rab Hannah, ended up representing the club and found ourselves playing the first game in the aftermath of a race riot!

Before each game over there, the reserve sides of the competing clubs put on a warm-up match. This one got the crowd going all right! We had gone into one of the townships to play against a side called Chibuku and Rab and myself wondered why an otherwise very trim stadium required wire fencing that was at least twenty feet high to be placed around its perimeter. We weren't long in finding out!

One of the coaches of our all-white side, who had taken umbrage at a late challenge made on our goalkeeper, had simply walked on to the pitch and flattened the offending player with a single punch. As all hell broke loose, the fans tried to scale the fencing to exact revenge, and truncheon-wielding policemen lashed out at the fingers of those

From Glasgow Celtic to the Salisbury Callies, Rab Hannah and myself are met on our arrival in South Africa by Danny Murphy and Dick Blackley (on the right).

trying to invade the pitch, sending them slipping back down the wire. I make no apologies for saying that, by this time, Rab and myself had quietly retreated to the relative safety of our dressing room and had locked the door in the interests of maximum security, suddenly feeling every inch of the many thousands of miles that separated us from home. Even at its most frisky, the Calton was never like that, though having seen the living and working conditions those people had to endure I could understand their volatile temperament.

That trip, though, would be the last time I would go to play football anywhere at club level without my Celtic team-mates for company. Three weeks before, Jock Stein had given me my first-team debut, replacing Paul Wilson as a substitute against Dundee at Celtic Park. The game was lost at the end of a season in which the club had failed to achieve the distinction of winning their domestic championship for a world record-breaking tenth time in a row. Significant changes were at hand and I was to find myself caught up in the middle of it all.

CHAPTER THREE

One Road — Different Directions

I played my first game for Celtic two weeks before Billy
McNeill retired and left the club. It would be three years
later, after Billy's return to Celtic Park, before I started to
blossom into anything like the player I had hoped to be in
the team's colours. In between were the years when Celtic
lost the twin pillars which had supported them as the
foremost side in the country. One was the foresight to
keep at least one step ahead of everyone else and the other
is what I would define simply as the will. In good times or
bad, the one constant feature of any Celtic side ought to be
a spirit that can not be crushed no matter how hopeless
any situation may look. There is no doubt in my mind that
my career would have progressed more quickly, and satis-
factorily, in a more traditionally settled environment at
Celtic Park. The fact that it did not is, not even now, a
cause for self-pity on my part. Players are pragmatic by
nature and out of the turmoil that engulfed the club in the
mid-seventies there arose for me at least the chance of a
regular game and the opportunity to play beside some of
these whom I regard as having been among the finest ever
to wear Celtic's jersey. As well as them, and to prove that
in confusion there can be profit, my professional life was
enriched by coming into contact at that time with an
assortment of some of the most colourful characters in the
club's history.

The name of Maurice Johnston would have to be
included among that number, even though there are Celtic
supporters who mentally erased the memory of his
association with our club after he 'jumped the dyke', to use
a well-known Glasgow expression, by joining Rangers. It

was the single most incredible transfer ever to take place within Scottish football, especially since Mo had been busily declaring his undying affection for Celtic two months before he turned up wearing a Rangers blazer and tie inside Ibrox. To be perfectly honest, though, I don't resent him one little bit for what he did. Having just gone into my own religious convictions, how could I, or any other person calling themselves a Christian, object to 116 years of bad tradition being broken? So far as I am concerned, Graeme Souness is to be applauded for taking on the bigoted element who support Rangers.

As for Maurice, it is probably some time since he was a practising Catholic but, whatever money he is getting from Rangers, he deserves it for putting up with the aggravation that will be with him all the days of his four-year contract at Ibrox, or until he decides to go elsewhere, whichever comes first. If a man who was born and brought up in Glasgow signs for a football club based in the city but is unable to live there with his family because he fears for the consequences, that is not what I would call a normal life. Mo is being handsomely paid to put up with the fact that two sides of the community despise him, meaning it would be unwise for him to live in their vicinity.

I don't feel bitter against a former Celtic team-mate who has gone over to the other side, though. A man has one life on this earth and he must live it as he sees fit. I would not sit in judgement on Mo and neither should anybody else, no matter how deeply they may feel a sense of betrayal. As for the so-called Rangers supporters who laid wreaths outside Ibrox on the day Mo joined Rangers, only idiots would do something as tasteless as that, anyway. Maurice, though, will be treated as an outcast on both sides of what we shall call the religious divide for the rest of his life and it is up to him to decide if the money he took from Rangers is worth that.

As a Celtic supporter and player, I am only disappointed that I was deprived of the chance I thought I was going to get of playing beside one of the great talents in Europe.

Let me go! I've just scored against Rangers. Frank McGarvey and George McCluskey aren't listening, though. Sandy Jardine is the unhappy Ranger.

The circumstances of Mo's decision to back out of his agreement with Celtic are unknown to me and most others, and will probably remain so. I was taken aback by some of the noises Mo and his agent, Bill McMurdo, made at the time and my sympathies are with the Celtic fans who must have felt it all added up to a hefty slap in the face. I still have all the time in the world for Mo, though, even if I do not hold with people professing their love for Celtic and then signing for Rangers.

As for the future, the signing of one Catholic-born player will not radically alter Rangers' status as the Protestant club in Scotland. Football doesn't change society in that way. Rangers supporters will watch their team with its new Catholic dimension once or twice a week. The rest of the time they can get back to feeling, and acting, as their inclination takes them. Unless, of course, Rangers, under Graeme Souness, really want to go for changing the social fabric of the country and start flooding Ibrox with Catholics, including schoolboys who still practise their faith. To do that would increase their support instead of Rangers losing anything except the extremist element.

By signing more Catholics Rangers would give themselves greater respectability in the eyes of those who wouldn't have followed them while they had a sectarian policy. The more successful the team becomes, the less the support will care about privately-held religious beliefs. Even some of those who were originally hostile to the idea of an open club might come back then as well. In the meantime, tension will rise at Old Firm matches while Mo is at Ibrox, or is allowed to feel as close as he will ever get to being comfortable there.

I would find it impossible to say whether Mo will be able to see out the duration of his four-year contract at Ibrox, or if he will have the inclination to do so. He has never stayed four years with any club since his career started at Partick Thistle and took him to Watford, Celtic and the French club, Nantes. There might even be a temptation for him to go for one more big move before he is too old, though it would obviously need to be outside Scotland. I am also not one hundred per cent sure that Mo fully appreciates all the implications of what he has done in going to Rangers, but I cannot find it within myself to despise him for what he has done. He has let down the Celtic supporters by his conduct but it's his life to do with as he pleases. Anything that can help reduce bigotry has to be a good thing, though Mo will derive none of the benefits while he is unable to walk the streets of his own city.

For this son of a Catholic father and Protestant mother, I'm only glad it isn't me. I have always known who my friends were and that is what sustains me no matter what Celtic are going through and that is what helped me to survive in my early days with the club when I was trying to make a name for myself.

In summing up the apprenticeship I served in the first team, during which time I played under Sean Fallon, Jock Stein and Billy McNeill in the space of three years, whereas Celtic had gone through the previous eighty-seven years of their existence using only four managers in all, I will attempt to recognise the contribution, and pay tribute to the influence, these men had towards constructing the player I ultimately became.

It should be stated first of all that I am, for better or worse, a product of the Premier League. Reconstruction of the Scottish League took place in time for the start of the 1975-76 season at a time when I had returned from Rhodesia and was looking to start making some headway in the first team at Celtic Park. In my opinion, the Premier League has grown increasingly worse so far as the percentage of genuinely talented players is concerned, to the extent that I would say ten per cent are gifted and provide entertainment and the other ninety per cent are suitably geared for an atmosphere in which it is only important that a team wins and the end always justifies the means. The same ten per cent, incidentally, turn it on every season, I've noticed. Games are won today by going out and biting, scratching and kicking to establish supremacy in the first place and, by so doing, create enough room for self-expression to finish off the opposition. It is no longer enough that any person has sufficient natural ability to get himself a game with any club side anywhere else in the world. In Scotland, that individual must learn to add more strings to his bow and I would use a present-day Rangers player as an example of what I'm talking about, namely Derek Ferguson. Derek was on the verge of being lost to Ibrox — and speaking on behalf of my side of the city of Glasgow, I would have to say I am sorry he wasn't! — because it took him a while to appreciate that he wasn't there just to play beautiful, constructive football, he had to become negatively minded as well and see that the other side couldn't score if they were a long way from his team's goal. Supporters are quite

Tommy twists . . .

right to say they would rather see the more refined touches
of those who have been immortalised, like the Jimmy
Johnstones and Jim Baxters, but if they had been around
in 1975 they would have been told they would have to
learn how to tackle a fish supper, and quickly!

Whatever reputation I have gained in the game, though,
it was not won by being physical. The affectionate chant
dreamed up by the supporters on my behalf which
declared that 'Tommy twists, Tommy turns, Tommy
Burns' is taken by me, with grateful thanks, as symbolising
that fact. It was also my undoing when trying to establish
myself at the time of Celtic's deepest crisis.

The car accident which almost cost Jock Stein his life in
the summer of that year left Sean Fallon in charge,
manfully trying to cope with profound loss and doing so in
the best way he saw fit, which was by being cautious and
not entrusting the team's fate to teenagers, no matter how
promising they had seemed prior to the start of the first
Premier League Championship. Some players, and good

. . . Tommy turns.

ones at that, never gave Sean the helping hand, or the respect, that he needed and for the first time since I was a primary schoolboy the club knew how it felt to go through an entire season without winning a trophy of any description. In total, I was given five league games, three of which were lost and one drawn, and I believe that was only at Jock Stein's instigation after he had started to appear at Celtic Park again after long months of convalescence. The fact that the team won the League and Cup double the season after that could be put down to extra dimensions having been added to it, even if, in the midst of that remarkable turn around, there was a sad oversight.

Andy Ritchie is a name that stimulates conversation and jogs the memory of those who saw him play and can recall some of the extraordinary goals he scored. He had the same number of first-team games for Celtic as me that barren season and was then allowed to leave the club, exchanged for a goalkeeper (Roy Baines), but was eventually destined to become Scotland's Player of the Year in

1978. For me, Andy's loss to Celtic was tragic because he was as skilful a player as Glenn Hoddle, and anybody who knows anything at all about the game will know that is a fair-sized compliment. He could have stood in the middle of the park and dictated the play for Celtic with that phenomenal passing ability of his, but the thinking was that big Andy was basically too lazy ever to amount to anything in the Premier League, which is a fair-sized condemnation of the type of thinking that had taken its hold on the game. Jock Stein could be very hard on his young players, and for him there was just too much nonsense in Andy's head. That much was certainly true!

Andy was not only the best singer I ever heard in a dressing room bath, he also smoked like a lum and was as mad as a hatter when the notion took him. For months, Andy was given his lunch for nothing every day at the City Bakeries shop at Parkhead Cross, just up the road from Celtic Park. He had gone in there one day and spun the ladies behind the counter this incredible yarn about him and his wife being homeless and with that big, angelic face of his they had taken in every last, deceptive word until his photograph appeared in the paper one day wearing a Celtic strip and suddenly Andy's slate was wiped as clean as his plate used to be at the City Bakeries.

Jock Stein was too serious about his football for that kind of behaviour to be tolerated, though, and there was too much hard work to be done for frivolity to be allowed. The manager had made his position, and mine, clear in an article he wrote for the club newspaper, the *Celtic View,* in which he said, 'One player who will start off the season in the first team is Tommy Burns and if he is good enough he will hold his place. Like so many of the new school of Celts, Tommy has loads of ability. Now he, and the others, have to show that their attitude is right, that they are worthy successors to the teams who have worn the Celtic jersey with distinction before them. But one thing the fans can be sure of is that there will be no passengers. Nobody will be taken along for the ride.'

A series of significant changes were made, the first of which was the remarkable coup of getting Hibs to sell him Pat Stanton when it had seemed big Jock might as well ask them for Edinburgh Castle and the esplanade while he was at it. It was no coincidence that Pat played in every Premier League and Scottish Cup tie that brought Celtic both those prizes. Removed from the middle of the park, where it was becoming more frantic with each passing season, and placed in defence where he could work the younger players about him as if by remote control, Pat made the ordinary performer look great. Sweeping as it may sound about a man who played a total of 44 games for Celtic, Pat Stanton has never been adequately replaced since he was forced to give up the game because of injury.

Rangers were already seven points behind Celtic in the championship, though, when Jock administered the *coup de grâce* by signing Alfie Conn to the stunned disbelief of those who had idolised him at Ibrox before he went to Spurs. I think Alfie had such a stubborn streak running through him he was actually able to make that move without worrying about the consequences. All I can say is, it wouldn't have been me if the chance had come to make the move in the opposite direction! With the arrival of Graeme Souness and, more recently, David Murray as the new owner of Rangers, I don't think there has ever been a greater willingness on that club's part to sign Catholics, as we have seen with the signing of Mo Johnston. Slow, but steady, absorption of Catholics into the side may follow. I would have to come clean, though, and admit that if, hypothetically, Rangers were to ask me I would not join them, and for the simple reason that I would have no inclination to put the depth of their supporters' bigotry to the test.

Religious division and that inbred mistrust of each other will always be there. I have been around it for long enough as a Celtic player to know that there are children on the street singing about 'Fenians' and 'Proddies' who aren't even old enough to know what they're on about. The one certainty, though, is that they will grow up to brainwash the next generation, and the Old Firm's rivalry in that respect will, consequently, exist in perpetuity. I couldn't join Rangers because it isn't just me I have to think about. There is my wife, sisters, father and mother to take into account and it would all be more than I could handle, even if I could come to terms with the idea of being Tommy Burns of Rangers in the first place! Deep down, too, I do not believe, no matter how liberal Graeme Souness and David Murray may be in their approach, that the majority of Rangers' supporters really want to see a Catholic play for their team.

Having said all that, I would be less than truthful if I didn't acknowledge that Alfie Conn was never fully accepted by a lot of Celtic supporters, and I have always liked to think that they are more open-minded and tolerant as a rule. Alfie, though, provided a tremendous lift to Celtic and players like myself in particular when he joined the team. Because Celtic are an open club, he was accepted gladly by everyone in the dressing room, too, and that included the one man it would not be possible for me to omit from the story of my life, the late, great Johnny Doyle.

When Celtic lost their way again in the season that followed the winning of the double, I thought it was as a direct result of signing players around that time who, through no fault of their own, were not up to the job of playing for the club. Jock Stein, too, had reached that stage in his career when he could have used some help, but when he looked about him there was nobody who could offer him the kind of assistance he required. Nobody had learned as much from working underneath him as they ought to have done. Jock still thought it was possible for him to sign players for small fees and then turn them into invaluable commodities as he had done a decade and more previously with people like Willie Wallace. Johnny Doyle would have to be exempted from the list of the inadequates, though.

Any goal for Celtic lifts a person off his feet and helps him walk on air.

The tragedy of Johnny's death in an accident at his home in 1981 has never diminished the man's legend in the hearts and minds of the supporters. Personally, it was a devastating experience for me because I like to think that I was especially close to him at Celtic Park. Many people had totally the wrong idea about Johnny Doyle because all they saw, or heard, was the aggressively confident, out-spoken and demonstrative side of him.

Inside Celtic Park, he would refer to Alfie Conn only as the 'currant bun', a particularly incisive piece of rhyming slang that would be provoked, humorously, by Alfie coming into the ground for training in the morning whistling 'The Sash'. Johnny actually thrived on the tension that surrounds the players of Celtic or Rangers and our supporters loved him dearly for that. There was no gesture too insensitive for Johnny to make, whether it was showing the crucifix he always wore underneath his jersey to the Rangers supporters or coming back to the centre circle after he scored a goal and performing the mime of flicking ash from an imaginary cigar in celebration. His rougher edge was not always reserved for the other side, either, because the two of us almost came to blows once on the pitch at Celtic Park in front of over thirty thousand people. After a mix-up involving our two selves, Aberdeen broke up the park and scored, which was more than Johnny could stand. The argument was so heated that a punch-up was definitely on the cards for our finale before we were both sent off, and we were only saved by the fact that the game was re-started, Celtic won a quick corner and I crossed the ball for him to score with a header. After that, we were in love again.

Johnny was a supporter with a strip and everybody knew it. He had a unique rapport with the crowd, and he knew that, too. On his way home to Kilmarnock after a game, it was not unusual for him to pick up hitch-hiking Celtic fans on the Ayr Road and take them into his house for a meal before they continued on the rest of their journey home. All the other stuff was a front to cover up for a mind that was never at peace. There were only two things that acted as any form of consolation to me after I came back from Johnny's funeral: the realisation that, at last, he was truly at rest and also that he had died while still a Celtic player.

Me and the late, great Johnny Doyle show our delight at winning the Premier League Championship. Dominic Sullivan joins in at Tannadice.

At the time of his death, Johnny was on the verge of being transferred but in life he was a Celtic man through and through and it seemed fitting to me that he should meet his death while still a Celtic man, and I know that would have been important to him, too.

Johnny and myself sat in the dug-out at Hampden when I won my first medal for Celtic, when we beat Rangers to win the Scottish Cup in 1977. It was a season of progress for me, in that I started twenty of the first team's games, but one of frustration as well, mainly caused by Hampden Park. Not to get on in the cup final left me feeling unfulfilled because I badly wanted to make my mark on that particular ground above all. Months before, Celtic had played, and lost, against Aberdeen in the League Cup final. It was my first appearance at the national stadium and I couldn't say anything other than the occasion got the better of me. In fact, I was taken off with twenty minutes left and replaced by Bobby Lennox, having spent the previous seventy minutes running up and down the park policing Dominic Sullivan, who was then with Aberdeen, while he watched my every move as well. I made myself the promise that day that when I got back to that place I wouldn't be beaten by my surroundings, no matter what else happened, but it would be another three years before I would get the chance to be as good as my own word.

By then I would have assumed more responsibility in the side, in any case, because Kenny Dalglish had gone to Liverpool and that left a huge gap that had to be filled as best we could. Kenny's last game was the Scottish Cup final I sat out and it was ironic he should have ended his captaincy of the club on such a high note against our oldest rivals. There was a popular myth among Celtic supporters that Kenny never did particularly well against Rangers and also a lot of resentment that he left the club when he did. Let me make it clear that, so far as this team-mate of his was concerned, Kenny was absolutely correct to get out when he did. He had done all he possibly could with Celtic and I think he knew that, the way things were within the place, his still untapped areas of potential were never going to be realised. At that time Celtic simply could not provide him with the quality of fellow player to complement his skills and Liverpool were also making a considerable impression on Europe, something we were far from up to at Celtic Park.

My salute to Danny McGrain, the best professional I have ever worked with at Celtic Park.

But for Kenny Dalglish and Danny McGrain, Celtic would have had to face up to certain harsh facts a long while before they had to confront the truth. Danny was the closest I have ever seen to perfection, both in the way he played his position of full back and in terms of the level of consistency he achieved over twenty years with the club. In all the time I have been with Celtic, he was the most complete player it was my privilege to work with. Of the current squad, Paul McStay is the one who has the ability to match Danny one day and earn that level of praise, but, for the time being, Celtic owe Danny more than they perhaps realise themselves. With Dalglish, he was a phenomenal worker, though playing on the left-hand side of them could be murder, since the ball rarely came your way. It would have to be admitted that they carried Celtic on their backs with that ferocious will to win that has to be a prerequisite of being a successful Celtic player.

That much became abundantly clear when, within the space of a few months, neither of them was there any more. Kenny's transfer was quickly followed by the lengthy injury to his ankle that took over a year out of Danny's playing life and, all of a sudden, Celtic's frailty was there for everyone to see. I have always thought that I would have been a much better player, for instance, had Jock Stein exerted a stronger influence over me when he was a younger manager. He was years ahead of his time as a tactician and that came home to me when, prior to his last season in charge of the team, Jock took us on a summer tour of Australia and we twice made short work of the Yugoslavian team, Red Star Belgrade. Stein's tactics were so simple when you thought about them afterwards but the looks on the faces of the Slavs as we forced them into mistake after mistake in front of thousands of their expatriate countrymen was priceless. They were foaming at the mouth trying to think of a way out of their predicament. Unfortunately, Celtic were left in a similar position when we returned home and promptly had our worst season for thirteen years, finishing up fifth in the league table, going out of the Scottish Cup to Kilmarnock, who were in the division below us, and losing the League Cup final to Rangers on the Hampden pitch that was definitely doing me no favours at all.

The well known firm (left to right) of Johnstone (Jimmy), Johnston (Mo) and Burns along with another old friend.

European competition has its own way of crystallising any side's shortcomings, and when Celtic went out of the European Cup to S.W.W. Innsbruck, who were hardly one of the aristocratic sides on the continent, the flaws were becoming indelibly marked. Celtic needed a figurehead who knew the club's traditions on an intimate basis and could communicate his pride in the club to the players at his disposal.

Billy McNeill was someone I used to watch get out of his car every morning for training at Celtic Park and expand his chest to its maximum measurements as he approached the front door, as if the air around the ground was more bracing than it was anywhere else. When he walked out on to the field on a Saturday afternoon and did the same thing in front of the other team's captain before tossing the coin for kick-off, there was this comforting feeling, whether you were playing or spectating, of knowing that there was a born leader at the helm. I had once cleaned his boots each day and whenever he walked into the room I was working in the aura around Billy McNeill was vividly clear to me, even allowing for the fact that I had been brought up as one of those who was taught to give the captain of Celtic the kind of respect that is reserved for people of regal bearing. In the summer of 1978, there was simply no other man who could have taken Celtic, and the problems of individual players, on board. I freely concede, too, that one of the first people he had to sort out was Tommy Burns who, while still trying hard to convince the sceptical that he was a player at all, had developed the unwanted reputation of being the classic redhead with the volcanic temper to match.

CHAPTER FOUR

The Fiery Redhead

The fights I had with Billy McNeill were caused by my foul temper and bad attitude and started off with the normal type of shouting and bawling that goes on between player and manager. Over the course of his first two years at Celtic Park, though, during which I was also busy letting myself down on the field by getting sent off three times, our arguments degenerated to the extent that Billy once had to fine me £200 and then, in a regrettable incident which still causes me to feel ashamed and embarrassed, the two of us had a physical scuffle in public at an Ayrshire hotel that I thought would end my career at Celtic Park. The story had a happy ending, though, because out of the brawl came an hour-long meeting in Billy's office that was to be the most informative of my entire career. It left me feeling that, for the first time since I became a professional player, the proper path to what the game could hold had been laid out in front of me, where previously I had been wandering about without any kind of guidance.

Billy McNeill took over from Jock Stein as manager of Celtic while I was on holiday in Houston, Texas with Bobby Lennox, who had gone there to play after leaving the club. When I returned to Glasgow, the trans-Atlantic flight and the time difference had played havoc with my body clock and I went into the ground to get sleeping pills from the man who was then our trainer, Bob Rooney. The new manager happened to be there and he took me out for a walk over the pitch, using my visit as the opportunity to start working, psychologically, on one of his players. In effect, Billy told me that, in the coming season, he wanted me to firmly establish myself in the first team and become what he called a household name. By the time he had finished speaking to the rest of the playing staff, Celtic had a team who were at fever pitch by August and would have done anything not to disappoint him or the supporters. Some of us, though, were capable of getting carried away in the process.

My problems with authority began a couple of months before Billy got to Celtic Park, in fact, when I was sent off for the first time playing against Partick Thistle at Firhill. The tragic thing was that I had already scored two goals in the first half of that game and was moving towards a very pleasing performance indeed when I clashed with Colin McAdam, whose brother, Tom, was on Celtic's side that night. We both chased a ball that went out for a throw-in which each of us thought was ours. Innocent enough, you might think, but it was an incitement to violent conduct so far as we were concerned. Colin's elbow was forcibly thrust into my ear and I freely admit that I retaliated by lifting my hands and aiming a blow at his face. I say 'aiming' because the intent was far more serious than the severity of the punch and I could only have grazed the chin of someone who was much taller, and much heavier, than me. Big Colin's head immediately started swaying as if he had been struck by a hammer and I was on my way to learning the first of a series of lessons on the subject of self-discipline. The referee was not impressed by either of us and showed two red cards, the first of which, I'm grateful to say, was pointed in my direction. I ran straight off the pitch into the visitors' dressing room with Bob Rooney for company and went directly into the shower to calm down, or so I thought. The next thing I heard was the sound of Colin McAdam trying to kick down the door, noisily telling everyone who was within earshot at the time exactly what he was going to do to me once he had entered the room the hard way. Bob Rooney, meanwhile, had turned the key in the lock and was standing in readiness to defend me in case it didn't hold firm. I can only wonder at what would have hapened if Colin had been sent off first and had been standing in the corridor waiting for me to come off.

The incident that changed how the public thought of me. Referee Hugh Alexander sends me off against Rangers in 1978.

An experience like that ought to have proved beneficial and mended my ways but nine months later, by which time Billy was in charge at Celtic Park, I got to know how it felt to be sent off in an Old Firm match.

The League Cup semi-final at Hampden was going Celtic's way when Rangers were awarded a penalty kick that was what the diplomatically inclined would have called controversial. My words to describe it were altogether less discreet and I fired them indiscriminately at Davie Cooper, who had performed a spectacular dive inside the penalty area, and the stand-side linesman, who had fallen for this piece of theatrical deception. I would maintain to this day, however, that at no time did I make contact with the Rangers player. The problem with getting involved in an incident of that type so soon after my scrap with Colin McAdam was that the general public's perception of me had started to change, and referees are

members of the public. I wasn't the only Celtic man pro-
testing vehemently to the linesman but I was the one
singled out by Hugh Alexander and sent in the direction of
the tunnel once again because I had a growing reputation
as a troublemaker. On that occasion Billy McNeill said, or
did, nothing to me, which was an indication of how he felt
about the incident that sparked off the trouble when we
were a goal in front.

The third, and last, time I was sent off, though, was when
the roof started to show signs of caving in above our
heads. I am not the paranoid type who believes that as
many refereeing decisions are given specifically to annoy,
or cheat, Celtic as some people would like to think is the
case. In September, 1979, though, when we played
Aberdeen in a league match at Pittodrie, even I was upset
by the free-kick award that had enabled them to take the
lead and my emotions ran away with me soon afterwards in
the first half when I clashed with Gordon Strachan. As the
referee reached up instinctively for his red card, I felt the
red mist descend and I decided in my obviously illogical
state that the best course of action to take was to strike the
match official with my jersey. As I started to remove it, my
own team-mate, Johnny Doyle, landed on top of me and
gave me some quick counselling with well-chosen words
to the effect that taking off, and therefore discrediting, the
Celtic jersey was not a fit response, particularly in front of
thousands of supporters who had paid a lot of money to
come a long way and see our more praiseworthy traditions
being upheld.

That was the mildest form of chastisement I was to get
over that particular incident. The newspapers pilloried me
for getting so carried away and demanded that the
manager do something about me and my violent
tendencies. In fairness to him, Billy did punish me, but not
in such a way as to prolong my uncomfortable stay under
the glare of the spotlight. I was fined £200, more than I was
getting paid in a week by Celtic at that time, and told in no
uncertain terms, though privately once again, that I was

fast turning into a liability at the club more than anything else. At that stage, I think Celtic could have sold me for about £30,000 and I don't think there would have been too much of a fuss. I was missing an increasing number of games because of recurring trouble with an ankle injury and the manager had told me that I was no use to him, in any case, because my fiery temperament was holding me back from making any progress when I did manage to play. It was all a far cry from the season before, when Billy had assembled a side of talented individuals, but not what I would have called an outstanding team, and inspired them to reach collective heights on a scale that was enough to win us the Premier League Championship. I had played in 28 of the 36 games during the winning of the title, more than anyone else apart from Roy Aitken, but the physical problem which has dogged me throughout my career forced me, unfortunately, to miss the one that really mattered, when Celtic beat Rangers in the unforgettable 4-2 game on our own ground after Johnny Doyle had been sent off but ten men won the league.

My damaged ankle has, at a conservative estimate, cost me two seasons out of my career for Celtic over the years and has been a source of frustration to me since I sustained the original injury in a reserve game against Hibs as a teenager. I've had two operations on the troublesome area and was told some time ago that the ankle is now arthritic. On the park it has affected my balance and made it difficult for me to twist and turn, which is supposed to be my trademark as well as a prerequisite of playing in the middle of the field. Afterwards, it has occasionally given me an excruciating pain but over the years I've learned to live with all of it. There have also been, from time to time, what I could only say were astonishing recoveries from discomfort and horrendous swelling.

The first time I was to be given the honour of captaining Celtic, which was the ultimate accolade so far as I was concerned, my ankle was grotesquely discoloured and had swollen to twice its normal size days before the game. Just

Acting as captain of Celtic means the highest honour a player can get.

walking normally to see the match seemed improbable. Coincidentally, I had taken into my house that week a special statue of Our Lady which had come from Italy and I said special prayers of devotion to it every night, asking to be given even temporary relief from discomfort as I was desperately anxious to be given that honour. By the weekend I was able to lead out Celtic and the pain had completely disappeared. On another occasion I was to have a third operation that was going to involve a complicated tendon operation but I had to delay entering hospital because of a severe bout of flu. Somebody was looking after me, though, because the aggravation mysteriously lifted and I was spared going through something that the surgeon had warned me and the club could affect my mobility so badly I would be struggling to continue as a midfield player.

Nothing could help me when I missed the climax to the

1978-79 season and when the injury problems persisted into the one that followed my reaction was to become even more cantankerous and unruly. I was, unwittingly, moving towards the day when my personal turmoil would come to a head in the most dramatic fashion possible. In all, I had played just twelve league games from the start and none at all in the Scottish Cup when the team went down to its traditional, pre-Hampden base at the Seamill Hydro Hotel on the Ayrshire coast to prepare for the semi-final tie in that competition, against Hibs. The afternoon before the game is the time when the tactics board comes out and the game is gone into in earnest. During the course of his introductory remarks about how Hibs should be approached, however, big Billy broke off to say that he felt it was terrible he should have to bring in a man of 35, Bobby Lennox, who had rejoined the club in September, 1978, to help put into the side the verve and enthusiasm that was needed for a game of such importance.

As he spoke, the manager's eyes scanned the room full of people in front of him wearing Celtic tracksuits, but when he voiced that particular criticism his eyes fell upon mine and the alarm bells went off in my head.

'Are you talking about me?' I heard myself say out loud. To say there was a stunned silence is an understatement. Even I couldn't believe what I had just done to someone who didn't brook argument from his players.

'If the cap fits, Tommy, you'd better wear it,' Billy replied after a momentary pause while everybody else shuffled their feet and fidgeted in their chairs, waiting to see what would happen next.

'Well, it doesn't,' I said, my voice beginning to tremble with emotion. At that point Billy blew up, too, and called for Neilly Mochan, one of Celtic's back-room staff. 'Neilly, you'd better get him out of here and back up the road,' the manager said, meaning my stay at the hotel was at a premature end and I was to be driven home to await further retribution. Even at that, though, I still wasn't finished.

'I'd be better off in the house, anyway, than listening to

this · · · · !' was my final word on the subject, the final word itself being extremely insulting and one I'm not proud of using. That was when the manager had taken enough of my insubordination and elected for an old-fashioned way of concluding our discussion. Out in the foyer of the hotel, in front of a huge fireplace there, Billy grabbed me by the throat and all of a sudden the gloves were off and the seconds were out. Johnny Doyle tried to remove the manager's grip on me and, once we were eventually separated, I was ordered to my room. I was there on my own for twenty minutes, quietly packing my bags and trying to come to terms with the fact that I had allowed myself to explode in a way that would surely finish my career with Celtic. No words could adequately sum up the feelings of shame and regret that filled my mind, as well as the worry I was going through over what to say to my family when the news got out.

Then there came a knock at the door and Danny McGrain, the team captain, stood there saying that Billy McNeill wanted to see me downstairs straight away. I told Danny that I expected to be sacked on the spot but he was supportive and told me there was always a way out of the darkest corner. It was Billy himself who showed me that it really is darkest before the dawn simply by speaking two sentences when we came face to face.

'Have you calmed down? Are you ready now to listen to what I have to say?' he asked. I nodded without being able to answer either question because of a sudden throat constriction.

The following day I came on as a substitute for my first Scottish Cup tie of the season and Celtic beat Hibs by five clear goals. At the end of the game Billy told me to be in his office first thing on the Monday morning. It was, without exaggeration, the conversation that changed my life. Billy put my entire career up until that point into clear perspective, beginning with his assertion that I didn't train hard enough on a daily basis to make anything of myself. When I thought about it, I realised that I had been kidding

Rosemary, myself and a few friends outside Saint Francis in the Gorbals after signing the most important contract of my life.

myself all along. Because I lived properly away from the ground by not smoking, drinking or staying out late at night, I thought I had no need to do anything else. It was pointed out to me by the manager, though, that I wasn't a naturally fit person and needed to work even harder than some others, in fact, just to maintain a reasonable level of stamina. All I could do was nod in agreement and promise to come in every afternoon from then on for extra training.

Next, Billy concentrated on my habit of giving in to minor injury and not playing on a Saturday when I thought I could get away with another week of living off my last good performance for the team. Remember, this was before my ankle had grown worse and, once more, I had nothing to say in my own defence against this charge of

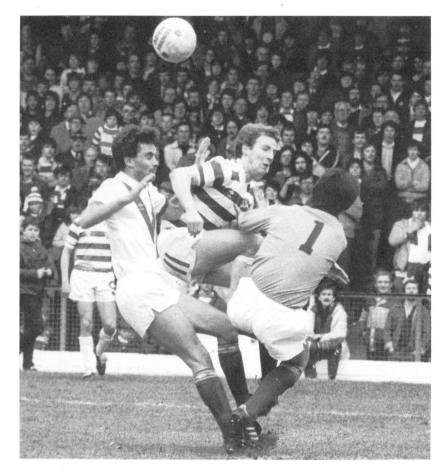

If you want to get anywhere . . .

malingering. I ended our meeting, in fact, by apologising
to the manager for my conduct in the team's hotel a few
days earlier and left that office a better man than the one
who had knocked on the door sixty minutes earlier.

Six weeks later I made the other crucial move of my life
when I married Rosemary at St Francis' in the Gorbals.
That completed the transformation of Tommy Burns.
From then on I had a sense of responsibility and stopped
the habit of looking after number one to the exclusion of
all others. Some people might have thought that getting
married at the age of 23 would be an added complication
in the life of someone with such a troubled past but I only

. . . you have to go in where it hurts.

wish now I had gone to the altar even earlier on. Leaving the Calton to go and live on the outskirts of Glasgow, in Newton Mearns, helped me create a little world of my own with Rosemary to which I could retreat and leave the cares of football behind. My family and friends were all mad about Celtic and it was all they ever spoke about. Rosemary's people were exactly the same, so it was a good thing to get away from all that and relax.

But for being put right by Billy McNeill and setting up home with Rosemary, I think it's possible I could have drifted about in my casual fashion at Celtic Park for another year and then left the club without getting more than a taste of what it really meant to be a player for them. The realisation of what I had come close to losing, and the appreciation of what I had to do in order to succeed, made me work all the harder and there were immediate compensations for such anguish as I had been put through. The only Scottish Cup tie I played from start to extra-time finish, as it happened, was the final itself in 1980, when we beat Rangers by the only goal of the game, scored by George McCluskey. My pleasure was heightened by the feeling that I had played well and overcome the mental block I had about doing well at the national stadium. The following season I had what I regard as one of my finest, sustained spells in a Celtic jersey, culminating in the winning of the championship by seven points from Aberdeen. I can't imagine it was purely coincidence that I should strike this rich seam of form at the time when I was putting into practice all the virtues of application and honesty that Billy McNeill had preached a year earlier.

My introduction to the Scotland Under 21 side had come along before then too. I played in the first-ever international at that level, in fact, against Czechoslovakia and would go on to get eight Under 21 caps in total before Jock Stein finally put me into the full international squad for the game against Northern Ireland at Hampden in 1981. Any youthful Old Firm player doing well in the Premier League is bound to get picked for the Under 21 side, although it's always good to get confirmation of your own rate of progress, but I always felt that my elevation to the full squad could have come earlier. Billy McNeill told me that Jock Stein, who was then national manager, was unsure of my defensive qualities. That argument for leaving me out used to rile me more than a little. If Jock Stein, or anybody else, wanted me to put in more work in that way, all they had to do was take me aside before a game and tell me what was expected. There would have been no difficulty following instructions, I can assure you.

I am the first to admit, of course, that playing for Celtic, with their attacking traditions, doesn't give a player like myself a great deal of practice in how to defend. Celtic are unique in their approach to the game, and it can sometimes be as frustrating as it can be gratifying to be a part of it all. The championship in 1980, for instance, was thrown away after we had taken a substantial lead over our challengers. It is a recurring theme where Celtic are

The first ever Under 21 game played by Scotland, against Czechoslovakia in Pils. I'm second from the left in the back row.

concerned, like the naivety and generosity we show in Europe (that same season we had two of a start on Real Madrid but couldn't hold it). In that particular championship, though, we turned negligence into an art form. On March 1, we had a ten-point lead over Aberdeen with a dozen games left to play. On May 3, we lost the title to Alex Ferguson's side by one point. The majority of our players wanted to get forward and win matches with a philosophy that, roughly translated, said, 'If they score one goal and we score two, what the heck.' Consequently, our recognised defenders were never put under regular pressure because we were superior to most sides. That was all very well until we met those who could make an impression on us, like Aberdeen, Dundee United and Rangers. When we had to defend, it was often every man for himself.

Since Billy McNeill retired in 1975, the perennial complaint has been that Celtic lack a commanding centre half. That isn't how I see the problem at all. What I believe Celtic have needed more than anything is a defensive

The first Scottish Cup winners medal for Roy Aitken and myself. It was 1977 and Celtic beat Rangers by the only goal of the game. Roy and myself put our heads together on how best to celebrate.

organiser, someone who wants to take part in the game and not wait until the other side are in our penalty area before acting. We need the kind of competitor who wants more out of the game than to make three good tackles and six good passes over ninety minutes. If I had been in charge of Celtic, the player I would have broken the bank to get would have been Willie Miller. A few years ago, Rangers thought about going after Willie when his contract was due for renewal at Aberdeen. I had this longing then for Celtic to break the bank and bring him to the club for five years. It would have been money well spent. Willie may not be the greatest with the ball at his feet but there is no better organiser or penalty box defender. Miller has an almost telepathic understanding of where trouble is going to occur next for his team and he would have left a lasting mark on Celtic if the initiative had been taken.

None of this is to denigrate the efforts of those who've played in Celtic's defence during my time with the club.

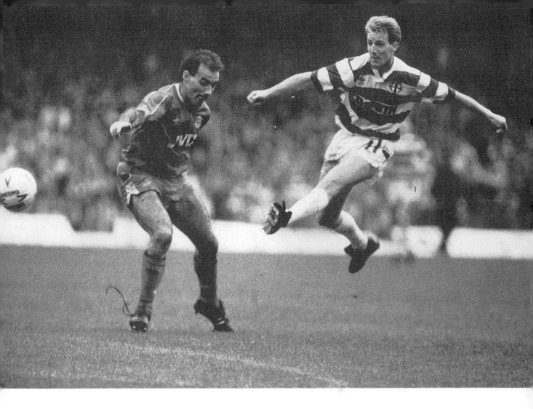

It's not often you find a way past this man, Willie Miller. I wish I'd had the chance to play on the same side as him — and I don't mean at Aberdeen!

Roddie McDonald, for instance, was as good as anybody when he had Pat Stanton beside him calling the shots. Roy Aitken, too, is an inspirational figure and a real Celtic die-hard. I have often felt that Roy would have been a world-class centre half had he had a Willie Miller type behind him. He did, remember, come into Celtic's first team as an outstanding young centre half but, because of circumstances, he has, as often as not, found himself sweeping behind the centre half. Celtic are always there or thereabouts at the top of the Premier League and we invariably score more goals than any other side during a season, but there are times when it would be good to mix realism with the romanticism and understand that we wouldn't necessarily be desecrating the memory of the club's past sides by building our attacks on a solid, defensive base.

The one piece of sarcasm that has always attached itself to Willie Miller has been his title as the best referee in Scotland. That isn't strictly true but, given the decline in standards among the members of that profession, it does have a basis in fact.

There have been games when I've had a good look at referees and wondered why they've chosen that line of work. For all that I had a tendency towards being a tearaway when I was younger, I don't accept that the pace of the modern-day game has made it any more difficult to handle. There is not one player in the Premier League that I would be afraid to tackle, and there are fewer con-men about than some people suspect as well. In 1989, though, two referees, Kenny Hope and Louis Thow, were punished by the S.F.A. for not being strict enough in their application of the rule book. Let me say this: Kenny Hope is one of the few good referees on the circuit and what happened to him was totally unjust. If the incident involving him and Willie Miller at Ibrox had resulted in the player using bad language that would have been indefensible. If an experienced professional, and therefore a grown man, speaks his mind in a non-provocative way, what's wrong with that?

The trouble with referees today is that not enough of them can handle the big crowds, and the attendant pressure, without feeling the strain. There ought to be more to their job than memorising the laws of the game. How these are interpreted, with the use of common sense, is important, too. That's why I was delighted to see Brian McGinlay restored to the Grade One list after the problems in his private life. He is the top referee in Scotland by the length of Sauchiehall Street. As I've said, there aren't as many referees with an ingrained bias against Celtic as some supporters would take for granted. In fact, life in general is not always what it seems inside Celtic Park, which is why, having done what Billy McNeill asked me to and establish myself in the first team while gaining

No matter how much hard work it takes, wherever it is, the effort is worth it to play for Celtic.

admittance to the national side, the time was not long before I did what most people, myself included, would have thought to be unthinkable. I asked Celtic for a transfer!

CHAPTER FIVE

Why I Almost Left Celtic

On three occasions in my life I have had to face the prospect of leaving Celtic. To the supporters with whom I have been able to forge a special bond over the years, giving into that temptation would, I suppose, have been, in their eyes, the ultimate betrayal of their trust.

These matters are never as simple as they seem, though. There is no word or phrase, for instance, that can adequately sum up the affinity I have with Celtic as an institution, and yet on most of those occasions when our relationship was strained, money was the root cause. I would prefer to say that the pursuit of proper financial reward, rather than the intrusion of greed, was at the centre of it all, though. If I make public here certain financial details of agreements that I have entered into with the club in days gone by, it is only in the interests of lending greater clarity to the understanding of those who believe that professional footballers are always on the make and that when they run out of ideas there is, invariably, a personal agent lurking in the background to provide some more schemes for a percentage of the takings. I am the Tommy Burns, don't forget, who once signed a contract with Celtic that involved me getting less money than the one I had agreed to four years before, and this is the same person who refused to have an agent because I wouldn't exploit my position as a Celtic player for profit away from the game.

So far as I'm concerned, I've always sold myself short when it came to Celtic. I have known that all along, and so does my wife. The quality of my life can't be quantified in pounds and pence, however, and while it is an old and very

Just champion! The League title is won at Love Street in 1986.

true saying that you can't eat medals, a person like myself can certainly take nourishment from them because of the happiness I have derived from getting six out of the Premier League championship, five in the Scottish Cup and one from the League Cup. In the end I know, just by looking at them, that I achieved what was most important to me in my life, which was playing well for my team, Celtic.

Equally, it is the case that the efforts I believe I have made on the club's behalf since coming into the first team in 1975 have only rarely been properly recognised by those at Celtic Park who are the ultimate judges of who gets what. In my own mind, I know I have contributed as much as anyone, and more than some, to what the team has achieved in the recent past. It may be that some will even regard me as a great Celtic player, while others will say I never reached the heights I might have done, something with which I wouldn't totally disagree. The truth probably lies somewhere in between. My assessment of my own career is that I became all the player I could be and won more medals than I ever dreamed of but still felt I could have been better if I had been surrounded by experienced players and a top-class coach. As it was, at the age of 25 I was one of the most experienced players, and have remained that way ever since. To my way of thinking, a player can only become truly outstanding at club level if he is constantly proving himself to be among the best in European competition. Celtic have never allowed any team that came after the legendary Lisbon Lions to do that because of a refusal to see that each successive season the side goes out of whichever tournament it happens to be in as a direct result of not having enough top-quality players in vital areas.

This is an ailment that can only be remedied by speculating on the very best players money can buy and then, hopefully, accumulating statistics more edifying than those which show that since I played in my first European tie, against Wisla Kracow in the U.E.F.A. Cup of 1976, Celtic have gone as far as the quarter finals of any of the major competitions only once, gone out at the first-round stage six times, the second round on four occasions and the third round on one other. We didn't even qualify for Europe in season 1978-79.

So far as the winning of medals is concerned, I believe I've been as successful as any Celtic player who came before or after the team who beat Inter Milan in the European Cup final in 1967, but the era of that marvellous side put them into the history books and left the rest of us to live with continual and unfair comparisons because that team will always be unique in the club's history. If someone at Celtic Park should happen to have no particular sense of the club's history or traditions, it would be possible for them to live with that.

One of the magical moments during Davie Hay's time as manager was winning the 100th Scottish Cup Final. I'm in between our scorers Frank McGarvey and Davie Provan.

I find it unacceptable that my passionate desire to emulate the supreme achievement of the past is sometimes not matched by others within the club. At times when we have needed the team to be strengthened, the good players within it have gone somewhere else instead, usually for a better wage. When more than adequate replacements have needed to be bought, stopgap measures have, in the main, been taken, making it look as if the club is settling for the occasional championship or cup win instead of setting their sights on attaining new heights.

For all that, there is a ferocity of spirit that makes me believe Celtic will always be able to beat any side in Europe on our own ground. If only we had about us Dundee United's organisation when not in possession of the ball, although in our double-winning Centenary year I felt we went a long way towards rectifying that. I have always thought that would be my perfect combination in Europe: Celtic's guts and flair, Dundee United's guile. When Dundee United lost the second leg of the U.E.F.A. Cup final at Tannadice against Gothenburg in 1987, a match I watched from the stand, they were only a goal down from the first leg of the tie in Sweden. The problem for me was that the Dundee United players seemed content only to make sure they didn't lose another goal rather than go out and win the game. What should have been their finest hour — and United had played brilliantly in the tournament up until then — was lost to them because caution let their heads rule their hearts. That attitude isn't normally associated with Celtic.

Typical of the kind of thing we get up to, though, was our progress in the European Cup the first season Billy McNeill had charge of the club. At one stage we were two goals down on aggregate against Partisan Tirana of Albania before stunning them, and a crowd of over fifty thousand at Celtic Park, with four goals in the space of twenty-four minutes, and all before half-time! In the next round there was a reprise of our long-playing fault when we scored three against Dundalk, from the Republic of Ireland, but somehow managed to lose two at home as well. This meant we had to live as dangerously as men on the run, which was what we had turned into, in the away leg. It was the quarter-final tie with Real Madrid that told the modern-day story of our lives, though.

At Celtic Park, we scored twice against the Spaniards and could have had more, but through the years I've rarely been confident with two goals of a lead whenever we go abroad to play anyone, anywhere, far less the legendary Real Madrid in the Bernabeu Stadium. Inevitably, we cracked under the strain, and there ended the best run I have known in Europe in all my time with Celtic.

Such frustration can fester in the system for a while and then create strong confusion about what to do for the best when, for example, an old contract expires and a new one is presented for your consideration. The dilemma facing me in the summer of 1982 was that I was being asked by Billy McNeill to commit myself to Celtic for the next four years. Ordinarily that would have been no problem but I was anxious then over whether I could spend those years productively enough at Celtic Park. As well as that I had just suffered the stunning disappointment of not being selected for Scotland's final squad of twenty-two players to go to Spain for the World Cup finals under Jock Stein, an episode in my life that I will explore in complete detail later on. Billy McNeill was, and still is, a shrewd negotiator.

Having once been on the playing staff at Celtic Park himself, I'm sure he was able to appreciate that my demands were far from excessive. In fact, he told me that, if it were up to him, there would be no need for any further discussion. In the background, though, I had the added complication of Terry Neill, who was then manager of Arsenal. He had contacted me, as he was entitled to do under freedom of contract, and said that if one of his players, Graham Rix, was sold to Italy, as seemed likely at the time, Arsenal would buy me from Celtic as his replacement. It was then I picked up a newspaper one morning to find Billy McNeill saying that if anyone wanted me they would have to pay one million pounds. Now, quite apart from the fact that I didn't believe any individual was worth that much money, I was taken aback to find that Celtic valued me so highly because my weekly wage then was just £200!

If I was worth that much on the transfer market, surely I should have been getting paid more by my present employers? This was the question that went over and over in my mind as the team left without me for a tour of Canada before the new season started. While they were away, Terry Neill called me again at home, but only to say that Graham Rix's move to Italy had fallen through and he would be staying at Highbury, which meant there was no place for me. More talks went on between the club and myself when they returned from North America and I can recall saying to Billy McNeill, who has always had my undiluted respect, that I still had reservations about a long-term contract in case he wasn't there as manager at any stage during its lifetime. He told me not to be so daft, I remember.

One year later, the unthinkable happened and Billy was out. By then, though, I had accepted new terms which gave me £300 a week and a signing-on fee of £18,000 that was to be paid in four, yearly instalments. My basic salary was not to be linked to the rate of inflation, either, but was to increase by twenty pounds a week at the start of each season. Consequently, when Billy McNeill came back to Celtic Park four years later, my wages still had not reached £400 a week.

That was to prove the most lucrative contract of my career. On average it has cost Celtic £3,000 a year in signing-on fees to keep me at the club since 1975, and even in total that represents a sum which has been bettered by more than one player simply agreeing to join Celtic since then and is one which I could possibly have doubled as a result of one, big transfer. In the end, I have allowed myself to watch others who have been at Celtic Park for a fraction of the time I have been there get more money than me for two reasons. In the first place, the events of the summer of 1982 and the other confrontations that followed were all decided by a quirk of fate outside Celtic Park which convinced me I was meant to play for Celtic and them only. Secondly, I consider myself to have been paid a living wage by the club for all of those years, one that has enabled me to keep my wife and children well fed and clothed and, so long as the team have won a trophy, provided them with a holiday every year. It is certainly not the case, though, that I'm set up for life, financially, and with my signing-on fees I have had to invest in a pension scheme that will help provide for the years after my playing career is over.

Winning the Scottish Cup, especially in the 100th final, is worth any bad break. Rosemary takes charge of the trophy on the night Celtic beat Dundee United.

Eventually, though, it will be necessary for Tommy Burns to go out to work like everybody else at some stage in the future. If that job is in football management, I know I will have benefited from the years that were spent playing under Davie Hay at Celtic Park, complete, as they were, with their highs and lows. It is essential to be absolutely honest in assessing Davie's time in charge for the simple reason that it was the most instructive four years of my life. I have already stated publicly that I do not think Davie was the right man for the job, but not because he was Davie Hay. There wasn't a young man anywhere in the world at that time who could have taken that post and given the support what they were clamouring for. The majority were unhappy at the sudden manner of Billy McNeill's departure, for one thing. I don't know the reasons behind that incident, so I can't comment, but what I can speak about is the period that followed.

Davie Hay arrived at Celtic Park to take over a squad

who had thrown away a nine-point lead in the Premier League Championship the season before, allowing Dundee United to take the title. That suggested to me the pool wasn't good enough by Celtic standards. There were rumblings among the support because it was the second time in four seasons we had blown a nine-point lead, Aberdeen having been the other beneficiaries. Billy McNeill had spoken to me on several occasions during that time concerning the fact that he felt the players were going stale. The majority of us had been together for six or seven years and he thought his team talks were not getting through the way he wanted. In hindsight, it may have been a blessing in disguise for Billy to have left the club when he did because his time in England with Manchester City and Aston Villa broadened his horizons.

Davie, on the other hand, arrived in 1983 to find Charlie Nicholas and George McCluskey gone to Arsenal and Leeds United, taking two top-class players out of a squad that was already short on quality. Frank Connor had arrived in advance of Davie, which puzzled me because I had always thought that a manager chose his own assistants. That is not a criticism of Frank, who had been with Celtic a few years earlier and had provided the team with the likes of Pat Bonner and Charlie Nicholas from a reserve side full of boys who loved him as much as he worshipped them. They were his boys and he coaxed and cajoled them until he got the best out of them. Frank was always good for a bit of banter when he came back to Celtic Park I think that was part of his trouble. Too many people still thought of him as 'wee Frank', the one who was good for a laugh, rather than giving him the respect his position as assistant manager warranted. Davie, too, needed to be successful straight away and that would have been a hard enough job for anybody, far less a man who, up until his appointment, had been to one game of football in the preceding twelve months. His every mistake was magnified a thousand times and while, initially, there had

David Hay arrives as Celtic's new manager.

been plenty advising him this way and that, especially over the choice of players to buy, the same people were eventually absolving themselves from blame and leaving Davie to take the flak on his own.

With the squad desperately short, Jim McInally was sold to Nottingham Forest and Brian Whittaker bought from Partick Thistle along with Jim Melrose, who had been in Coventry City's reserve side, and John Colquhoun, from Stirling Albion. If I live to be a hundred, nothing will ever convince me that Davie made those signings off his own bat. Quite simply, he was ill advised where an experienced manager would have known that when you lose quality you have to replace it with players of equal, if not superior, merit.

Celtic should have sought someone like Jim McLean or Alex Ferguson, whose knowledge gained by having been over the course before would have been invaluable. It could be argued that Jim had been given the chance to join Rangers at one time but had opted for the security of the corner shop, as he calls Tannadice, therefore he might not have taken the Celtic job had it been offered to him. Fergie might have taken it, though. So far as I know, his father used to run a Celtic supporters' bus in Govan and his son had never hidden his admiration for Celtic's style of play or the backing they got from the crowd.

Having said all that, Davie had a unique style of management in that he was relaxed and very much his own man. Football certainly wasn't an obsession with him in the way it was for the Fergusons and McLeans. To be an aspiring young Celtic manager going through the learning process, however, it was necessary to eat, sleep and drink the game, as he ultimately discovered. Davie was a real player's man, though, and he listened sympathetically to a request for the bonus system to be reviewed soon after taking the job. We were far from being a greedy bunch of players because we had been taking the same league bonus money for seven years while the club had gathered huge fees for Charlie Nicholas and George McCluskey to mention but two. The players, and Davie, thought we were due bigger incentives, but we were wrong. The directors of the club at that time let Davy, the players and, most importantly, the supporters down badly by a total lack of ambition on the transfer front and no incentives given to the players. It was due only to our love of Celtic and the supporters that the team, though not good enough, contested every competition to the death in true Celtic fashion.

In the balance against Rapid Vienna. Celtic should not have agreed to play the Austrians at Old Trafford on UEFA's instructions.

But in spite of finishing runners up in the league and losing finalists in the League and Scottish cups, as well as having some memorable results in Europe, like the 5-0 defeat of Sporting Lisbon, we had won nothing and that adds up to failure at Celtic Park. Davie accepted the blame for that but, in fact, he performed a minor miracle with that squad of players, given that it was short on quality replacements. Some may say Brian McClair, bought from Motherwell, was more than adequate but any decent goalscorer who is played at centre forward by Celtic should, in my opinion, score 20 to 25 goals every season. In any case, a lot of experienced quality was needed to stimulate the Provans, McGrains, Aitkens and Burns but, instead, Celtic signed those who looked to us for guidance. The pressure was on us all the time to win matches but far too much was demanded of the players I've mentioned. Most of that group were in the 24 to 26 age bracket, a time when we should still have been learning but for us there was only frustration as the entire club seemed to stagnate. There seemed to be no ambition beyond squeezing the last drop of flair and imagination out of players who could do nothing about it as, one by one, we all suffered. Personally speaking, I went through the worst season of my career and, being as much of a Celtic supporter as a player, I was disgusted by what was going on inside the club. As a Celtic player, it is wonderful when the team is winning trophies but torture when you're going through a hard time.

In my case, it seemed everywhere I went people were asking me what had happened to Tommy Burns, and that went for television, radio and newspapers as well. Davie Hay, to be fair, was very supportive at that time but others seemed to think I had a magic wand that could be waved every week.

By the end of that season, and particularly because of the build-up to our cup defeat by Aberdeen, things had deteriorated to the extent that I decided to ask for a transfer. I had worried myself sick over my lack of form and progress and God must have been sick of the sound of my voice as I prayed for strength to get me through the torment I was suffering. Since he was the manager, I thought Davie should have had the answers to why I had lost all consistency but, looking back on it, he was in-experienced enough to be looking for a few answers on his own behalf.

The approach to the Cup final was the last straw. For the umpteenth time, Davie had a talk with the players about bonuses, promising us that this time there would be a recognition of the game at Hampden being Celtic's last chance to salvage something out of an otherwise barren season. We were at Seamill to prepare for Hampden when the manager told us the day before the match that we were, in fact, to get the biggest win bonus ever given to any Celtic side if we came back with the cup. After our final team talk, the atmosphere was, as you might expect, electric until Davie said each man would get £2,000 for a win. A deathly hush fell over the room as a squad of

Happy days at Old Trafford. Sometimes it was not so good on Manchester United's ground.

players who had been together long enough to remember any worthwhile bonuses let the shock set in before Danny McGrain, the captain, said, 'Boss, there must be some kind of mistake. That was the bonus we got for winning the cup against Rangers four years ago.' Davie's face betrayed a mixture of embarrassment and shock. I could have wept for him because he had been left exposed in front of the players he was supposed to handle. Most of the team felt the same way because we quickly hushed up the whole affair and resolved to go and get the cup, anyway.

I have never felt as proud of being a Celtic player as I did on that day, in spite of the fact that our ten men (Roy Aitken had been sent off) lost to an Aberdeen side who were, tactically better than us. We gave them the fright of their lives and I can still close my eyes and see Fergie jumping up and down in the dug-out as we tore into them. When I looked at the Celtic supporters singing and dancing as if we had won the cup, I also thought to myself, 'Where will I find people like these anywhere else?' Thoughts of a transfer had become a reality, though, after the let-down of the night before. It gave me no pleasure to add to Davie Hay's worries because the knives were already out for him but even he said he understood my reasons for wanting away. He told me in no uncertain terms, though, that, while he was sympathetic, he expected me to honour my contract because he couldn't afford to let any players go. Since I wasn't looking for a fight, only a sense of direction in my career, I accepted his answer and left his office determined to have a more consistent second season under him, while hoping Davie would make some moves to strengthen the team. Had I been one of those players who passes through Celtic Park with the intention of picking up a few quid and then going on their merry way, I wouldn't have bothered my backside about the club's problems but I was, and I am, first and foremost, a Celtic supporter.

I was also taking the club's difficulties home with me and I'm sure it did me no good to play every game at that time as if it were a public trial. Davie was always telling me not to be so intense but you are what you are and I couldn't help myself. I didn't think I had suddenly become a bad player. On the contrary, I still thought I was the equal of any midfield player in the country but for a few years my career had been on the rise and now I was finding out how Tommy Burns handled adversity. The season that followed was a bit better but I was still in a rut and only climbed out of it when we managed to win the Scottish Cup against Dundee United.

I was substituted that day when there were still 25 minutes to go and I was followed not long after by Paul

McStay. How many managers, already one goal down in a Cup final, would have the nerve to do that? Davie Hay did and I can honestly say that, in spite of that, there wasn't a happier person inside Hampden than me when the final whistle blew and those two, late goals from Davie Provan and Frank McGarvey won us the cup. At the end of the day, it is more important Celtic supporters all over the world have a reason to celebrate than it is for Tommy Burns to have a good game.

At that time, Chelsea let it be known they were interested in signing me, but once again Davie told me that he could not contemplate letting anyone leave after selling Frank McGarvey and John Colquhoun. The only way I could be sold, he said, was if Celtic were successful in getting Leeds to sell them Frank Gray. I left the ground that day and went straight to St. Gabriel's church to kneel before Our Lady and ask for guidance. The following day, Davie called me into his office and my stomach immediately began to churn. The message was brief and to the point. The deal with Leeds had collapsed and Davie wanted to know if I wanted to become Celtic's new left back. I could have kissed him! I had played there before under Jock Stein and Billy McNeill and I knew I could do the job. I went straight back to church to offer my thanks for being shown that it wasn't a change of club I needed but a change of position. The next season proved to be my best for three years, culminating in the winning of the League Championship one magical day at Love Street against St. Mirren. I couldn't have been happier, though it was typical that the people who were screaming for my head were then saying that I was being wasted playing at left back and turned their attention, and abuse, to Paul McStay. Paul took a long time to find consistency under Davie Hay but those years will be of help to him if he ever hits a slump again.

For myself, it is still irritating that what should have been the peak years of my career were spent feeling frustrated. A player should always be learning, no matter his age, but all I learned was more about myself as a man. I don't blame Davie Hay for any of that because I watched him with great admiration as he constantly came back for more in spite of endless criticism. I just wish the people who had appointed him in the first place had sat down and really thought about what Celtic needed. Instead of getting a tried and tested manager, they elected to sacrifice a young man whose sole credential for the job was that he had once been a very good Celtic player. Davie's partnership with Frank Connor started well enough but deteriorated to the extent where, two and a half years later, they were miles apart in ideas and personality.

The end for Frank came suddenly at Celtic Park, but not before somebody was able to telephone Radio Clyde with an exclusive story. We were playing Dundee at Dens Park that day and before, during and after the match the air was full of talk of a sensational development about to take place at Celtic Park, though the full story was never broadcast. I was told that night by a close family friend that Frank was to be sacked but he was called to the ground the following day still unaware of what half the country seemed to know. If I ever get the chance to meet the person who gave Radio Clyde that information, I would take great delight in putting one on their chin for the hurt and embarrassment they caused the family of a good Celtic man. After winning the title, I thought about Frank and how he must have felt. I said in a radio interview afterwards that I thanked God for answering my prayers, and that was meant as an indication of how badly I wanted the championship for the supporters, the players, Davie Hay and Frank Connor. I know that, no matter what, his heart is still, and will always be, at Celtic Park.

One year after that beautiful day at Love Street, Davie had gone as well and the club's handling of that episode left a lot to be desired because a true Celt deserved better. I had suffered the worst injury of my career against

Dynamo Kiev and spent a worrying few months on the road to recovery. In the dressing room I was aware of talk among some players about contracts they intended to take up with other clubs six or seven months later. We won nothing that season and I often wonder if that was because those players were saving themselves for what they considered to be pastures greener. One or two, in fairness, always gave their all but some did not and Davie Hay's career as Celtic manager was cut short by their performances. Strangely enough, the last few months he was in the job saw Davie exhibit a different side to his character. He became harder to satisfy where his level of expectation was concerned and discipline was tightened up considerably.

His decision to appoint Tommy Craig was also inspirational because the development of players like Paul McStay, Peter Grant and Derek Whyte since then has been breathtaking. Tommy has also given someone like me a new hunger for the game.

Sadly, though, in his quest to bring new players to the club, Davie was told that he would need to buy them out of his own pocket. On reflection, I would live through the Davie Hay years again because I found out an awful lot about myself and about others whom I had once respected. Some people might think I have gone over the top with all this talk of frustration, saying that, after all, it's only a game of football we're talking about. To a Celtic supporter, though, the team is a way of life. If I hadn't been able to turn to God and Our Lady at that time, I think I would have put my head in an oven. Without those four years I might have never got as close to God as I feel now and so, ironically, those were the years I learned about life. But what no-one has known until now is that I almost quit the club, and football, just a few weeks earlier after yet another disagreement with the club over money. Throughout that season, as Celtic doggedly went after Hearts while people outside the club kept telling us we were wasting our time, I felt I had been making my most significant contribution in years to the team effort. Going to full back had given me a different perspective, and when I went back to midfield later on it was with a fresh awareness of what was going on around me.

Agreement had also been reached in principle between Davie Hay and myself over the signing of a new, two-year contract. To my dismay, however, he came back to me and said the club could not give me what had been agreed upon. I know that he was just as disappointed as I was about that but, once again, he had been overruled. The offer I was made to renew my contract contained no rise in a basic wage and a signing-on fee that was £4,000 less than the one I had been paid before. I was so taken aback I asked the manager to convey to the club my feeling that they would know what they could do with their offer. Four years earlier, I had been promised a testimonial match by our late chairman, Desmond White. The contractual offer was, I felt, designed to make me stay on at a reduced rate of pay, knowing that I would not walk away from my own benefit match. At the time I had an offer from a friend to go into a line of business that would have meant giving up playing altogether. With hindsight, I don't think I would have ever gone through with it, but at the time I was outraged and angry enough to think about it. I even called one of my old confidants, Frank Cairney from Celtic Boys club, and told him what I intended doing. It was Frank who brought me to my senses. Frank told me, in the old-fashioned way, that, in light of that, there was no way I was going to cut off my nose to spite my face. I went back and signed on again, taking the gamble that nothing would happen to me in the intervening years, like a loss of form and a transfer elsewhere. Not for the first time, though, the actions of the club had left me mystified.

Let me tell you a bit about testimonial matches. They're usually given after ten years' service to one club, but there are no hard and fast guarantees. What about those players,

The game is full of ups and downs and I'm about to experience the latter against Partick Thistle.

too, who can have seven outstanding seasons and then have their form shade off for a while, causing them to be released when they might have been thinking they were in line for a benefit game? That has happened at Celtic Park to men like Tom McAdam, Roddie McDonald and Murdo MacLeod. I would like to put on record now, though, my gratitude for the outpouring of affection that was shown to me by over forty thousand people when Celtic played Liverpool in my honour. The supporters showed me what I had meant to them and it was a day that was worth one hundred contracts or a million hassles over terms. It was a very moving experience to know that I had a place in their hearts and, so far as the faithful were concerned, a legitimate place in Celtic's history. We were united like a family that day, which always encourages debate on why the ordinary supporters can't be made to feel as if they have something to contribute towards the club on a more tangible basis.

The question often asked among the supporters is this: when are Celtic going to go public and let the people invest their money in the people's club, an organisation to which they have devoted their time and support? A lot has been said in reply about the possibility of Celtic falling into the wrong hands, the club passing into the control of the fat cats in other words. Surely, though, a system could be devised whereby a share issue that would allow fathers to buy their way into the club without gaining control, and with the ability to pass their shares on to their children, is not contrary to principles or visions of how Celtic's history should progress. Nobody has a greater respect than I have for Celtic's tradition and I believe that Rangers, for example, will lose some of their magic in the eyes of the people who follow them because the club is now all about big business and not the object of their supporters' dreams and aspirations. What I envisage is an opening for those with Celtic leanings to feel an even more welcome part of the family, which would also help the club generate the finance to buy new players and strengthen the team.

Celtic will never be able to match Rangers for commercial revenue, but that isn't what it's all about for our fans, anyway. If, sometime in the future, the club would open up it would make so many people happy and make their desire to see the club prosper even more intense. I regard myself as a typical Celtic man: if they bleed, I bleed. The club has about it that something special and magical which inspires a consuming passion for its welfare. At least you know where you are with that kind of emotional commitment, too. When a Celtic player is called upon by Scotland to play for his country, the feeling of all being in this together can sometimes be less than strong.

CHAPTER SIX

Celtic and Scotland

Someone, somewhere, has a blue, two-piece suit with the S.F.A.'s official crest on the breast pocket that was made to my specifications. They will have had it since I left the thing on a bus in 1982 and never even thought to go back and ask for it. When it came to Scotland's international side and me, that was the only thing that was ever tailor-made for Tommy Burns. Between 1981, when I made my full international debut against Northern Ireland at Hampden, and 1988, the occasion of my last cap against England at Wembley, I accumulated the grand total of seven appearances. Even at that I never managed two games in succession and my own overall impression of my international career, if you could call it that, is that I often wondered what I was doing there when I was called up to represent my country. Most of the time I was left feeling embittered and frustrated as I was overlooked in favour of other players in a way that reinforced a long-held suspicion of Celtic men, namely that entry to the national side is less accessible to players from our club than any other.

There has been a history of discord between Celtic players and those who choose or support Scotland's national side that long pre-dates even my birth and it is something that is worthy of considered exploration. It is a fact, for example, that Jimmy McGrory, a man whose goal-scoring exploits entitled him to be thought of as one of the genuinely legendary figures in Scottish football, never mind just a Celtic Great, could not get a game for Scotland at Wembley or many other places and finished his career with only 7 caps. Why?

Bobby Evans, a highly influential force at Celtic Park in

the late forties and throughout the fifties, once took a drastic step of writing to the S.F.A., asking not to be considered for the Scotland team because he was disgusted over being persistently rejected in order to introduce a varied, and sometimes unusual, assortment of others. Why?

Jimmy Johnstone, respected the world over before and after he was a member of the Celtic team who won the European Cup in 1967, finished his time in the game with 23 caps to show for his efforts on Scotland's behalf, 27 short of the number it would have taken for him to gain admittance to the S.F.A.'s Hall of Fame. Jimmy was also the first Celtic player to have his so-called fellow-countrymen denounce him from the terracings at Hampden so that the crowd could see him replaced by the player of their choice. Why?

David Hay, my former manager at Celtic Park, was once described as the 'Quiet Assassin' by Tommy Docherty while he was in charge of the national side, a form of compliment meant to convey the effectiveness with which Davie sorted out Scotland's most dangerous opponents. Davie, though, was another one who was knifed in the back by the mob in a fit of misplaced patriotism so that the people's preference could be promoted to the national stage. Why? I will tell you why, because eighty per cent of those who actively support Scotland by turning up at Hampden and paying their money are Rangers men through and through. Contained within their number you will find the more extremist element who would rather have a Scotland side that contained no Celtic players at all, while the rest give the impression that they would rather not be placed in the position where they would have to show some sign of appreciation for the contribution made by the players from our club.

It is a state of affairs that still exists. Roy Aitken, who is Scotland's captain and widely respected by his inter-national team-mates as well as Andy Roxburgh, Scotland's National Coach, finds his efforts go almost totally un-

D

recognised by the ones who would tell you that, as Scots, we are all basically Jock Tamson's bairns. Some of the children are bigger favourites than other members of the family, however!

The explanation is a simple one, so far as I am concerned, and represents the social history of Scotland over the last hundred years in microcosm. However distasteful it may sound, Scotland is a country that is still divided by religion, and these so far irreconcilable differences extend to the national football team. By and large, Celtic supporters do not share the fervour of the Rangers following for Scotland. One look at the traditional Celtic end of Hampden on the night or day of any international match will provide conclusive, visual proof of that. This has to do with their own family background, a sizeable percentage of them being the grandchildren or great-grandchildren of the Irish immigrant population who arrived in the West of Scotland near the turn of the century. The more radical wing of the Celtic support would, let's be completely honest, rather see the Republic of Ireland doing well, as they proved by their attendance in support of Eire during the European Championships in West Germany in 1988. This has everything to do with their own ancestry and because, to their way of thinking, Scotland, and therefore its representatives on the football field who form the metaphor for life in this country, stands for something they do not on a cultural and theological basis. Hearing Celtic players of the past and present being vilified when they're doing their best and being discouraged when valid claims for the inclusion of others from Celtic Park are ignored has inspired the continuation of that antipathy.

None of this is to say that players like myself are, or were, indifferent to the prospect of playing for Scotland. When it came to wearing a dark blue jersey, I was as chauvinistic as the next guy. I just never got the chance to prove it that often, that was all. The man who saw to that in the main was, ironically, a former Celtic manager, Jock Stein.

A sight that was seen all too rarely for my liking; playing for Scotland — on this occasion against Northern Ireland in 1983.

If Jock was trying his best during the years he was in charge of Scotland to prove to everyone that he was totally impartial, then he made a bad job of it by going the other way and working against the interests of some of his former players, and I would definitely include myself among them. My unused suit was left, still on its hanger, inside the coach that was to take Scotland's team away from Hampden after the defeat by England in May, 1982. On that day Jock announced his squad of players, twenty-two in all, for the World Cup finals that were due to begin in Spain two weeks later. I had been included on the list of forty players that was to be whittled down, along with Roy Aitken, Davie Provan, George McCluskey and Danny McGrain. Ten days after achieving that distinction, I was chosen to play against Wales at Hampden in the first game of the Home International Series and thought I gave a good account of myself, raising my own hopes at the same time that I would make the final cut. In spite of the fact that Scotland won, the team was changed for the next game, against Northern Ireland, and I was put out, destined not to return. I missed the game that came up against England the following Saturday, but as I sat in the stand watching the match beside Davie Provan I remarked to him that Scotland's display was so bad it might turn out to be a blessing in disguise for both of us.

By then there were twenty-four players left from whom two would have to drop out. Why the final squad had to be named that day while we were all gathered at Hampden, I do not know, but the way the news was broken to us turned out to be deeply embarrassing for me. Jock Stein came into the dressing room, in which all two dozen players were congregated, and started giving out details of the travelling arrangements for the World Cup party's departure.

'Obviously, not everybody is going. Tommy Burns and Ray Stewart will be staying behind,' he said. That was it.

A severe disappointment that would have been hard enough to take if we had been spoken to in private or even written to by the S.F.A. was turned into a public broadcast. I remember glancing over at Ray and seeing that, by the look on his face, he was as stunned and disturbed by what had happened as I was, only he was trying not to let it show. The last place either of us wanted to be, though, was in a crowded dressing room with those who were going to Spain coming up and offering their condolences. I felt like a schoolboy whose mother hadn't turned up to collect him and when I eventually got out of the national stadium I took one look at my lightweight suit on the bus and walked straight past it, having decided that I wouldn't be needing it, then or in the future. I drove to meet my family still seething with anger, determined to let it be known on an official basis that I would not be interested in playing for Scotland ever again.

Not to play in the World Cup finals, wherever they're being held, causes a feeling of profound loss to any player who thinks he's good enough to grace that stage and put up his credentials for the most stringent examination of all. In 1982, I was an established member of a Celtic side who had won the Premier Division Championship three times in the previous four years. To my way of thinking that should have counted for something, particularly for a left-sided midfield player. That was one position for which there was no abundance of alternative choices in Scotland's case, and yet the most peculiar lengths were gone to in order to find one, ensuring that I was kept on the substitutes' bench or out of the reckoning altogether. The total number of caps I have for Scotland in no way reflects what I achieved during those years with Celtic, and that's something I find hard to take. When I think back on some of the slights I have had to put up with, I can only conclude that I didn't get a fair crack of the whip when it came to being selected for Scotland during the time when I most deserved to have my form recognised.

There was a time when I sat looking on as a spectator at Wembley and watched Asa Hartford, a midfield player, being forced to come off the field against England because of a broken arm. His replacement was David Narey, who has never been considered anything other than a sweeper with his club side, Dundee United. Believe me, I'm not blaming Davie, who is an excellent player, or anyone else who has ever come before me in a Scotland context. On reflection, I think that part of my problem always revolved around the fact that Jock Stein went through his life thinking of me only as 'Wee Tommy', the groundstaff boy who came from down the road in the Calton and used to look after the towels in the laundry at Celtic Park after the first team had finished training. I never felt I got the full respect I was due from Scotland for the efforts I had made to improve myself at Celtic Park while Jock was there, or after he had been succeeded by Billy McNeill.

I am not suggesting, though, that I was the only one who suffered that way at the hands of Jock Stein or those who assisted or came after him as Scotland manager. Two of the most glaring examples of people who had to withstand a similar fate were Rangers players, in fact. Robert Russell was one opponent for whom I had the highest possible regard because of the intelligent and entertaining way he tried to play the game at all times, but he was never capped. Davie Cooper was another who wasn't used anything like as often as he should have been. Davie went to Mexico for the 1986 World Cup finals and was used for ten minutes. That was ridiculous when you consider that Scotland went through that tournament scoring only one goal in four and a half hours of trying against Denmark, West Germany and Uruguay. Surely Davie would have provided a more direct threat to the opposing goal than was ever evident elsewhere.

That was Alex Ferguson's decision. He took over after Jock Stein died and his record with Scotland did not make impressive reading. That is why I will say the S.F.A. were correct in what they did when they altered Scotland's managerial profile and went for the more methodical approach of Andy Roxburgh. Andy gets criticised for a variety of trivial reasons but I can't find anything wrong with his credentials for the job. Much is made of the fact, though, that he didn't manage a club side. All I can say is Jock Stein and Alex Ferguson were two of the most celebrated managers in the history of Scottish football and achieved nothing other than qualification for the World Cup finals. The trouble with the Scottish psyche is that we either build people up to knock them down or refuse to give others an even break because we don't like the look of them.

We are also badly stereotyped in our thinking. A manager must have a pedigree that starts with him going down a pit or else coming from the depths of the Second Division, where he learned to work on a shoestring budget. Players must conform as well. A right back must be a right back, a centre half a centre half and nothing else, as if it were a football game behind a glass case in an amusement arcade. That isn't how it works in the more sophisticated, and successful, countries throughout the world. Take Italy as a case in point and think about their central defender, Baresi, who can link up with the front players or end up taking corner kicks if necessary. He and others like him want to lend themselves to the game, and until we bring that more liberal dimension to our style of play we will be kidding ourselves that we can seriously compete at international level with Scotland, or in the major club competitions with Celtic or anybody else. Andy Roxburgh is a man of cosmopolitan tastes in football, who has taken the best ideas from his travels throughout the world and moulded them into his philosophy on the game. If he can't modernise Scotland's thinking, nobody can.

The general public have this immovable image of Andy as someone who was once a headmaster and can't get out of the habit of treating his players like schoolboys. When I won my first Under 21 cap against Czechoslovakia in 1977, Andy was in charge of the side and doing the things that got him a bad name with those who wondered about someone who gave his players Mars Bars to eat before a game and also played them cassettes of songs like 'Scotland the Brave' and such like on the bus going to the ground and in the dressing room before kick-off. Eating chocolate for energy, though, is a perfectly sound, medically approved, idea, and since when did Scotsmen object to a bit of spirited singing to whip up feeling?

What has brought down more public scorn than anything else on Andy Roxburgh where Celtic supporters are concerned, though, is the case of Frank McAvennie and his supposed rejection by Scotland's National Coach. Frank and Andy came back on the same aeroplane from a friendly international against Saudi Arabia in 1987, went their separate ways at Glasgow Airport and have never been re-united since in an international sense. But I wouldn't accept Frank McAvennie being included among the list of Celtic players who have been hard done by over the years by those responsible for choosing Scotland's team. While nothing has been said officially, it's common knowledge that there was an incident between manager and player on the aircraft carrying the Scotland team and this has caused the breakdown in relations between the two of them. Not having been there, anything I said about the exact nature of the trouble could only be considered hearsay. What I can do, though, is offer my opinion that, whatever went on, Frank's behaviour would not have seen him cover himself in glory. In other words, I'm saying that Andy Roxburgh has been wrongly pilloried a long time over Frank McAvennie. No manager needs to put up with a disruptive influence within his squad if he can possibly avoid it, no matter how good the wayward player in question may be. Frank, make no mistake about it, is very good indeed. I would say he's possibly the best all-round front player I have ever worked with, and that list includes Charlie Nicholas, Maurice Johnston and Brian McClair.

Frank's lack of professionalism lets him down at times and I would put that down to not getting a proper example to follow as a young player. Anyone who has failed to notice that Frank likes a social life hasn't been paying attention, and if they think that doesn't make any difference, then all I can say is they're wrong. Frank McAvennie has 'blown it', and it's time to stop blaming Andy Roxburgh for what has gone unaccomplished by him with the national side of which Frank should have been an integral part.

Coincidentally, it was the National Coach who gave me my last Scotland cap, against England at Wembley in May,

1988. Andy will never know what that meant to me because I had badly wanted to get another international cap to give to my youngest child, Michael, who had been born ten months earlier. As Celtic went through the first half of the club's Centenary year steadily making sure of winning the League Championship and moving towards the Scottish Cup final as well, my confidence grew, and when I was eventually called into the squad to go to London I was mentally and physically ready to give of my very best. I would also have to say that, after my bad experience with Jock Stein six years before, Andy was also very thoughtful in the way he handled my introduction to the squad after a long absence. I was taken up to his room the day before the match and told that my return to the international scene would actually have come about eighteen months previously had it not been for the fact that both times Andy went to see me play I got badly injured. I left his hotel room feeling on top of the world, and yet on the day of the match I was disappointed to find myself listed only as a substitute. Once again I was second fiddle to such as Neil Simpson of Aberdeen, who had spent most of the season recovering from injury, and my former Celtic team-mate, Murdo MacLeod, a member of a team, Borussia Dortmund, who had finished a lowly twelfth in the Bundisleague.

I had never played at Wembley before and I badly wanted to experience the feeling, so I spent my time constantly warming up on the perimeter of the pitch, staring in the direction of Andy Roxburgh and trying to transfer my thoughts about getting on into his mind. Eventually, I did appear but at a time when England were already a goal in front and there were only 15 minutes left for play. My feeling was, and still is, that Paul McStay and myself had proved we had an understanding cultivated with Celtic which could have been helpful if it had been used from the start. Sometimes, though, Scotland go out not to lose games rather than demonstrating adventurousness and attempting to win them with a bit of flair.

Having said that, I would like to get another chance to play for Scotland and I don't consider that unthinkable, either. When players get to thirty years of age, there is a rejection of them, subconscious or otherwise, on the basis of being too old to have anything left to offer. There are plenty of examples that can be offered, however, to contradict that theory. The Dane, Morten Olsen, is still one of the best defenders in the world, for instance, and he was thirty-seven when he played in the last World Cup in Mexico. Given the right game and circumstances, I wouldn't consider another cap as being completely out of the question for me. The current Scotland squad have, under Andy Roxburgh, developed a harmony that makes it easy for a newcomer, or a returning old boy, to settle in. This makes them a lot more determined looking than the first full international pool of players I was involved with in 1981. At that time it seemed as if a bunch of experienced names came together, played a match, and said 'Cheerio' to one another. Andy Roxburgh is a patriot who has fostered exceptional team spirit. His biggest job, though, will be to re-educate players and supporters alike, getting them to accept his vision of how the game should be played. Under Andy, though, the days have gone when it was harder to get out of the side than it was for some players to get a game in the first place.

If the same thinking had applied when I was looking to make an impression at international level, I would have chosen to play beside the one man who might have assisted me to become a regular, Graeme Souness. If I had been in with him, Gordon Strachan and John Robertson from Nottingham Forest, that would have been my idea of a Scotland midfield.

Graeme, of course, is not the favourite person of any Celtic supporter. He wasn't exactly an idol of the Rangers support, either, until he became the manager at Ibrox and started to be thought of as the greatest player who ever lived. Regardless of who thinks, or thought, what, Graeme was an outstanding person to have on your side. On a personal level, I have always found Graeme to be a very nice man who, in spite of his obvious wealth and style, never forgot that he came from ordinary beginnings in Edinburgh. At the same time, he does have that split personality that would enable him to stand on my leg while making a tackle and look straight through me.

We played on the same side only once, and that was in a nondescript match in Canada during a Scotland tour there in 1983. To this day, I'm convinced Jock Stein only took me there to make up for what happened between us at the time of the World Cup the year before. The game itself was played on a synthetic surface that was so bad it reminded me more of a car park, but Souness still gave his all and no-one will make me feel embarrassed, as a Celtic man, about giving out credit where it's due, even if the recipient is manager of my club's historic rivals for the last hundred years and more. The Old Firm will remain fundamentally divided for another century, too. That is why it is necessary to put the clubs, and what they stand for, into some sort of perspective, because Celtic and Rangers are not just two rival football teams but distinct cultures.

CHAPTER SEVEN

The Cause

When anybody takes on Celtic, they're taking on something that is genuinely unique because it means confronting players, management and supporters who are held together by what I first heard described by the manager of Aberdeen, Alex Smith, as 'the cause'. I have yet to hear the emotional commitment to Celtic summed up in a more explicit way. To my mind, there is no room for misunderstanding. My interpretation of the term is that it is not politically biased and meant to signify an affiliation with old, sectarian conflicts. It has, instead, everything to do with an appreciation of being the underdogs in our own country, a minority group who are bound by a hereditary link with the tradition that brought Celtic into being for humanitarian reasons and therefore made them different from any other football club. It is a feeling of common purpose that sustains the team and supporters alike and makes us as formidable as we are, particularly in times of adversity. The only way the cause can be taken to be politically orientated is that we, the Celtic players and fans, have been formed into our own union in which unity is our strength.

The night Alex Smith summed it up so perfectly was at Pittodrie, four days after we had suffered a 5-1 mauling from Rangers and tried to leave their ground with as much self-respect as possible under those circumstances. After going two goals behind to Aberdeen, the Celtic support, who had used up every ticket for the match regardless of what had gone before, were still behind the team every difficult step of the way and we came out of the game with an honourable draw. To those on the outside, all of this

The Cause — and its effect. Celebrating with the Celtic fans after beating Dundee United to win the Scottish Cup and complete the 'Double' in our Centenary year.

might sound like romantic nonsense, or even paranoia as some people like to call it. However, Celtic supporters are also unlike any others in Scotland because they support only one team. They do not have two scarves of different colours and possess a split personality which enables them to follow the team of their choice — and whoever happens to be playing Celtic.

As important as trying to define here what Celtic stand for is to declare my understanding that we are on our own and that the majority in this country would rather Celtic were not successful. Even in defeat, though, it ought to be essential that we conduct ourselves in a proper manner. I would certainly like to believe that Celtic supporters, unlike others, are not mean-spirited people who would want the team to win at all costs. That is the reason why our club can travel anywhere in Europe, or within Britain, and know that Celtic's good name will not be besmirched by bad behaviour. We must also accept whatever comes our way at home, on or off the park, with the same demonstrable show of togetherness. When we lost the Scottish Cup Final of 1984 to Aberdeen in extra time, after playing with only ten men for most of the time, I remember sitting at home that night and taking telephone calls from friends who told me how proud they felt to be Celtic supporters because of the way the crowd had willed on the players and we had responded by playing like men who had additional reserves of energy. The team are very much aware, too, of the empathy that exists under the heading of 'the cause'.

In 1983, Celtic lost the Premier League Championship on the last day of the season because of the two points won by Dundee United against Dundee at Dens Park. At Ibrox, meanwhile, we were two goals down to Rangers in a way that looked like adding insult to injury until they made the fatal mistake of delaying taking the field after the interval. As we stood out on the pitch waiting for them, the players got a chance to stop and look at the wave of support for us behind one goal. That is a breathing space you don't often get in an Old Firm match, and by looking at this mass of humanity singing, pointing and generally jumping up and down, it was possible to feel the fresh surge of energy run through the team. By the time the game kicked off again, Celtic had been sufficiently motivated by the cause to run Rangers into the ground, and the four goals that we scored could have been more. As Billy McNeill said afterwards, if you have to lose the title, that's the way to do it.

Not for the first time that night I heard people say, 'Never mind the result, what about the crowd.' These people are psychologically stimulated by being in each other's company, feeling that they are among kindred spirits and knowing that the power they can generate is tremendous. Celtic, let's be completely honest, are regarded as being the organisation that represents the Catholic community, but it is not only about the club remaining faithful to a past that started with the team being formed by the Irish immigrant population. The bulk

Happiness is . . . wearing a hooped jersey and celebrating the winning goal at Ibrox. Rangers 1, Celtic 2, 5th November 1983.

of our support ranges from teenagers to those in their mid-twenties and I don't accept that they're exclusively Catholic, either. What do they know about Ireland and all that? For them, supporting Celtic is something that has been handed down from generation to generation, their birthright, and it's something that is largely based on backing a philosophy about the way in which the game should be played. That is certainly the way it was in my family, and once you're in the union, it's a lifetime membership.

In 1979, when Celtic won the league title in the now legendary 4-2 game at Celtic Park, I was out of the team because of my recurring ankle injury. The stand was full to the point of overflowing that night and I found myself seated in among the fans and totally absorbed in the atmosphere, singing along with, rather than being inspired by, the Celtic support. Any Rangers supporter looking over from his side would have had all his suspicions about Tommy Burns confirmed for him that night! The Celtic fans are special, even if people occasionally get the wrong idea about them. When the team has had to go out on to the park at the end of games that have been lost at Tynecastle, Ibrox, Love Street or Pittodrie to wave to the crowd because they have refused to disperse, it is a gesture that is seen by those who are not Celtic-minded as a hollow act of defiance designed to disguise disappointment. That is not what it's all about, though.

It is, in fact, a demonstraton of imperishable spirit. They are what they say they are: Celtic supporters, faithful through and through, and they have their reasons for being that way, too. The truth is that the support believe that in order for Celtic to be successful they have to beat more than just the other side.

Where referees are concerned, I think the supporters suspect that bias is occasionally shown against Celtic during matches. More questionable decisions go against us than any other club, according to them. Perhaps it doesn't happen as often as some of the more excitable fans think it does, but it does go on with sufficient regularity to be disturbing for some others. They think there are other referees who, in order to prove that their particular background has not influenced them in favour of Celtic, bend over backwards to show their impartiality and end up being unnecessarily harsh on the club. There are plenty of examples to illustrate why there is room for saying all of these things, too. When a referee by the name of Kevin O'Donnell handled a league match between ourselves and Hearts in 1987, for instance, there was widespread controversy over his decisions at Celtic Park. This concerned the fact that the referee did not award Hearts a penalty kick they felt they should have got in the first half of that game and also his decision to give Celtic a goal, scored by Mark McGhee, when the Hearts players claimed he had committed a foul before putting the ball in the net. The events of that night effectively ended Kevin O'Donnell's career as a referee. After an official complaint was made by Hearts to the S.F.A., he was ultimately demoted to the rank of linesman and subsequently resigned from the governing body's list of officials.

All I ever wanted out of life was to see Tommy Burns in this jersey.

Later on, when two other referees, Kenny Hope and Louis Thow, were criticised for their handling of games involving Rangers and Aberdeen because they didn't send off two Pittodrie players, Neil Simpson and Willie Miller, they were immediately in trouble as well without the need for an official complaint. Both of them were banned by the S.F.A. from handling Scottish Cup ties, even though the Scottish League refused to have anything to do with sanctions being imposed.

During Davie Hay's time as manager of Celtic, he was especially forthright in his comments whenever he felt the club had been unfairly treated in that way. Davie was only echoing the views that were held by the ordinary supporters of the club but he wasn't given the backing from within Celtic Park that he deserved. After one game at Easter Road Davie actually came right out with it and stated that he felt there was one rule for Celtic and another for the rest. He also drew attention on another occasion to what he felt was undue pressure being exerted on the referee, Bob Valentine, before the 1984 Scottish Cup final between Celtic and Aberdeen, the game in which Roy Aitken became only the second player in the history of that competition to be sent off at Hampden during the decisive match. Davie continued to speak his mind, too, and after Celtic had lost to Rangers in the League Cup final two years later because of a disputed penalty kick six minutes from the end, he finally went for broke by saying that Celtic should have come out of Scotland and applied for membership of the English League if we wanted to get natural justice. The manager was condemned for expressing those sentiments, but I can only say that over the course of my career there have been times when I have felt that we were being treated harshly in many games.

A prime example was a game against Rangers at Ibrox in 1977 when our centre forward that day, Joe Craig, was blatantly knocked to the ground inside the penalty area and the entire Celtic team froze on the spot waiting for the referee to do the correct thing. Instead of that, however, he waved play on as if nothing had happened and let Rangers run off, unchallenged, to the other end of the park and score the goal that brought the game to the brink of anarchy. How many times have Celtic been a goal in front, too, only to be denied what seemed to everyone like an obvious penalty kick?

There was a time at Tannadice when just such a situation arose and a one-goal lead for Celtic turned into a defeat after we had been disrupted by not being given a penalty that was so clear-cut that only a blind man, or someone with tunnel vision, could have missed it. Whatever misguided notions anyone might have had about Davie Hay being a quiet man, incapable of angry outbursts, would have been shattered that afternoon. He was at the referee's door with that faraway look in his eye that was the signal to duck and it took a fair bit of persuasion, I can tell you, to get him away again without making his feelings known in the sternest possible way.

Whenever incidents like that arise, Celtic supporters feel that the press in Scotland are generally slow at coming forward in defence of the club, while being insatiable in pursuit of their vocation when it comes to having a go at us on other occasions. This is not true of all journalists, of course, but some do seem to take a great delight in high-lighting anything that they think shows up the club in a bad light, for example transfer stories without foundation which have, over the years, undoubtedly undermined morale at the club.

For instance, some time ago there was a long-running controversy over the fact that some Celtic players make the Sign of the Cross at times during matches. The matter came to a head when we lost the League Cup final to Rangers in October, 1986. Seven Celtic players were booked and Maurice Johnston, of all people, was sent off, blessing himself as he went to the tunnel. The match was so torrid, the refereeing decisions so contentious and Maurice's actions so controversial that Celtic's board of directors felt compelled to issue a statement on the affair the very next day. It said:

'Some aspects of the Skol Cup final left us as a club feeling rather aggrieved, but there is nothing to be gained by going over them in detail.
Most people who are interested in football either

saw the game or watched it live on television and they know the reasons for our dismay.

We want publicly to praise the behaviour of our fans throughout the game for the fantastic encouragement they gave the team and for exemplary conduct.

Some Celtic players allowed their emotions to get the better of them, particularly in the closing moments of the game, and that is an area which the club will deal with internally and privately.

We will not, however, allow the club to suffer or be deflected by any amount of adversity from any source. The events at Hampden will strengthen the resolve of everyone at Celtic Park to create a team good enough to overcome all obstacles to our ambitions.'

The words were dramatic and far-reaching, but there was only a tacit reference to what Maurice Johnston had done and that was just as well because his Sign of the Cross could not possibly have been taken seriously.

Here he was being sent off, with the massed choir of the Rangers support chanting, 'Cheerio, Cheerio, Cheerio', and Maurice, by virtue of moving his right hand from his forehead to his chest, and then from his left shoulder to his right, causes tens of thousands of people to splutter and change their tune to one about him being dirty, Catholic and illegitimate into the bargain. With all due respect, I had to laugh. Apart from anything else, not least of which is his present playing address, Maurice may have his own privately held religious beliefs but in any word-association test Faith is not what you would automatically put after his name. I will accept, though, that gestures, religious or otherwise, are never clever in the context of an Old Firm game for fear of any irrational reaction they could inspire among an easily provoked crowd. That is why Ibrox is the one and only ground where I would not make the Sign of the Cross. Rangers' ground, magnificent structure though it may be, is a citadel in the eyes of our supporters. It represents the home of a people who are everything they are not and an organisation of which they want no part. That is why Celtic supporters should not be inflamed beyond the state of high excitement they are in when they enter the stadium.

Anywhere else, though, I reserve the right to conduct myself as I see fit. The making of the Sign of the Cross would not rate a mention in newspapers or any other form of the media if we were playing in any country outside Scotland, and I would not give a guarantee here that I would never bless myself on the park if I felt like doing so in the future. I would not be dictated to by anyone over this matter, either, because, for me, the practice of my religion is far more important than any football club. To make the Sign of the Cross is not to indulge in an act of provocation, it is a demonstration of faith, whether you happen to be Brazilian, Italian, Polish or Scottish. After the statement made in the wake of the League Cup final, there was no move made by the directors at Celtic Park to visit the dressing room and lay down hard and fast rules over players blessing themselves, and that was as it should have been.

If Pat Bonner, as he does from time to time, makes the Sign of the Cross to ask for God's protection in his goal, is that a bad thing to do? Chris Morris blesses himself when he runs on to the park, craving the same indulgence. Where is the harm in that? The first time I can remember doing it was against Sporting Lisbon in a European tie at Celtic Park in which we started two goals behind on aggregate. I scored the first of our five goals that night and it arrived so early in the match I knew we were going to be far too strong for the Portuguese. In my excitement, I ran towards the touchline and it seemed a natural thing for me to make the Sign of the Cross and offer up thanks for what had just happened. It may also have been the first time a player was ever criticised for blessing himself at Celtic Park after he had scored against the side wearing the green and white hoops! Sporting Lisbon, of course, wore Celtic-style jerseys, but it is the case that some former Celtic players, when asked to give of their best against their old club, have difficulty in doing so, which also highlights the attitude of mind that shapes the cause.

Frank McGarvey, for instance, has frequently worked himself to a standstill in games against us since he left Celtic Park in 1985. What is he to make of it all, though, when the crowd at Celtic Park are singing 'There's only one Frank McGarvey' and cheering him on to the park? I'm certain that, subconsciously, this causes the problem of being unable to perform as freely as he would in other surroundings. And this is a man, don't forget, who saved Celtic's bacon in 1985 by scoring the goal that won the one hundredth Cup final only to be told a matter of days later that he was being put up for sale. In my opinion, Frank was treated abysmally by the club at that time. Celtic, though, is still an institution in the eyes of the supporters who attach an almost mystical significance to the team and all its works. That is why I have always felt that whenever Celtic win a major trophy the squad of players responsible should be presented with their medals on the park in front of the supporters.

Any side who had, since 1975, won a total of eleven domestic honours would have been immortalised. In the post-Lisbon era, however, the impression has been given that those associated with the club take these achievements for granted. I don't believe the fans would see it that way now. Celtic is a fusion of the players' will and the crowd's resilience. If the day ever dawned when I had to face the prospect of playing against Celtic, I would do so willingly because it would mean that I could at least be back among those fans once again. Whatever happens to me in the future, I will always be Tommy Burns of Celtic, both in the minds of the supporters and in my own. That is not something I have to live with, it is something I would not have any other way. I know that during whatever times of bad form or niggling injury I have had to endure the

Cue singing and dancing; my goal coming up against Rangers.

I think the expression is, 'How do you like it?'

supporters have stood by me because they appreciate having one of their own kind out on the pitch, and I don't mean that in any overtly religious way, either.

In spite of anything I have said elsewhere about Celtic and the vexed question of money, there is one thing I can say with complete sincerity and that is that the club owes me nothing. They may have had me for less than they should have over a long number of years, but at the end of the day it was still my pleasure. I know, too, that my children will help form the next generation of Celtic supporters. It has never been my way, or my wife, Rosemary's, to go on to my family about what their daddy does for a living. They know all the words to all the songs just the same, because Celtic is something that is passed on like an heirloom, and if I don't tell them, their aunties and uncles will.

The slightly frightening thing is that after 1992, and the proposed free movement of labour that will do away with transfer fees, players may lose any sense of loyalty to one club or its ideals, simply moving around looking for the maximum return on the skills they have to offer.

Unless the European parliament can be made to realise how damaging that legislation could turn out to be to the good of the game, the long-term future of some clubs could be in jeopardy. Football ought to be treated as a special case, otherwise we'll get to the stage where the individual with six months to go on his short-term agreement will suddenly stop trying too hard in case he gets hurt and spoils his chances of another move elsewhere. There is only one place where the damage caused by an act of parliament would not be irreversible, and that is Celtic Park. Celtic is an institution as well as a football club. It is what represents the hopes and aspirations of a particular people, the team's self-esteem corresponding perfectly with theirs at any given moment. Every win is a blow against those 'forces' the directors at

Celtic Park were talking about in their statement in 1986. Each trophy won is also tangible proof of having overcome the 'obstacles to our ambitions'.

It will remain, therefore, the ambition of countless youngsters to grow up and wear the green and white hoops. Those not fortunate enough to do so will then support them in continuing the cause.

CHAPTER EIGHT

Our Debt to Rangers

Rangers have set the agenda for the game of football in Scotland during the 1990s and it's up to the rest of the country to adjust, and react, to what is going on, both the people involved at administrative level and those on the terracings who have to realise that certain rules and practices are being re-written while they look on. First of all, though, it should be said that we will possibly never fully appreciate the debt that is owed to Rangers for doing what they did to reconstruct the face of the game, and I make no apologies as a Celtic man for saying that. It is precisely because I had eleven years' experience in the Premier League before Graeme Souness came over from Italy to be manager at Ibrox that I can make these comments so sincerely. I can honestly say that I was beginning to feel jaded because of the repetition involved in playing the same clubs four times a season, over and over again. There must have been somebody at Ibrox who felt the same way before coming up with such an imaginative idea as asking Graeme to come and play professionally in his own country for the first time and also deciding that money should be no object once he got here.

The millions of pounds that have been spent by Rangers on bringing household names into the Premier Division have, so far as I'm concerned, re-activated my interest and enticed their rivals to broaden their horizons at the same time. Would there be so many internationalists of cosmopolitan backgrounds playing in Scotland now had Rangers not acted as the catalyst for change? I don't think so. Players respond to the quality of the opposition they have to face and I have felt revitalised since 1986, even if it means working hard at keeping myself in a state of finely honed fitness in order to keep up with the greater demands that are made of players at the highest level. For me, that means another brisk training session on my own after the normal day's work at Celtic Park is over.

My body has to be thought of as an ordinary workman would consider his bag of tools, and that means keeping everything sharp. There is a programme of abdominal exercises I use to ensure that, whatever else happens, I will have the stamina provided by the body's engine room to keep up with the ever-quickening pace of the Premier League. If that is what it takes to keep me a part of the first team at Celtic Park, it is a small price to pay. Price being the operative word in more ways than one as the game moves towards the next century.

Everyone connected with Scottish football is in the process of being re-educated in financial matters. When Rangers were taken over by David Murray and started employing people like Alan Montgomery to attend specifically to the club's commercial activities, the game took off in a new direction. From now on, for instance, it isn't how much money a club can make through the gates on a Saturday afternoon that will be important so much as how good they are at raising revenue in other ways from Sunday to Friday. This kind of business acumen is what will decide in future how successful any club will be on the park. And when Rangers can generate millions of pounds at a time — that proves how drastic are the changes that will have to be made elsewhere to keep pace, let alone overtaking them.

It goes without saying, too, that the present-day players will demand their fair share of the new wealth that is being created, and that is where the supporters are going to have to come to terms with a changing world as well. Those players who are talented enough to rise above the more basic aspects of the Premier League and help maintain the game as an art form, and therefore a major spectator sport that is also attractive to advertisers, will want the maximum pay for the services rendered.

Footballers are no different from any other species of working man, and why should they be? Also, if you're with one of the Old Firm clubs the pressures, and the level of expectation, are that bit higher as a consequence of being constantly in the limelight. The most contentious issue in the eyes of Celtic's supporters in recent years, for example, has been their frequently voiced disgust over what they see as players who are supposed to have the good of the club at heart, and make a regular point of saying so, yet who end up leaving. The role of personal agents in all of this can drive the fans to distraction as well. I have never had, or felt the need for, an agent but I would not deny them or the job that they do because I genuinely believe they are entitled to their place in the modern game. Perhaps I should qualify that by saying that if they behave in a reputable fashion there is no harm in any agent acting on a player's behalf to provide the professional advice he is entitled to take over contractual negotiations.

When Maurice Johnston left Celtic in 1987 there was an outcry at the time because the supporters felt that he had walked out on his responsibilities to the club. My point of view on that would have to be that Maurice saw out the lifetime of his contract and did so while being subjected to the extraordinary problems that living in Glasgow can bring to a Celtic or Rangers player, therefore he was, in my eyes, above reproach. Maurice was a high-profile personality who was susceptible to public harassment and suffered abuse of his property along the way, too. He did see it out to the bitter end, though, and it is surely the inalienable right of any worker to assess his next move and perhaps take up other employment once he has finished a contract with one firm, even if they are one half of the Old Firm. If he is offered conditions that he finds more favourable elsewhere, even if it is Ibrox, then it stands to reason that individual is perfectly entitled to go where he wants without disagreement.

The moment I knew I had taken my place in the Club's history. My first look at the crowd before my Testimonial match.

I would also mention that when I met Maurice Johnston a year after he had left Celtic for the French club, Nantes, when we were both members of Scotland's squad to play

England at Wembley, I could detect a pleasant change in his general demeanour, and one that was definitely for the better in respect of his own peace of mind. In saying that, it would have to be stressed that Celtic did everything that was humanly possible to satisfy his financial demands, contrary to what anyone may say or think. The club also did all that they reasonably could to compensate for Maurice's decision to leave by breaking Celtic's record for an incoming transfer and signing Frank McAvennie from West Ham. Within eighteen months of arriving in Glasgow, though, Frank was back in London and that was unfair.

If a person agrees to terms that were good enough to entice him to sign a three-year contract in the first place, the honourable thing is to see out that agreement in its entirety. However, Frank said he was unsettled and so was his fiancée. In that way, he again ought not to have been different from the men who work away from home, if that is what Frank considered London to be. If his place of work was in Glasgow, then that is where Frank's girlfriend, Jenny, ought to have been with him, or at least understood from afar that this was where he had to base himself. In the case of Frank McAvennie it could be said that the agent who also acted for Maurice Johnston, the much talked-about Bill McMurdo, did Celtic no favours by his handling of the affair.

In general terms, though, Celtic supporters will now need to realise that what they have held to be sacrosanct, the ideal of playing for the jersey above all else, is, however regrettable it may be, something that may not apply in the future.

Playing for Celtic has always been enough to satisfy my needs because they were the only club I was ever interested in playing for, and I would trust that the supporters have always appreciated that was the case. This has also been true of some of the players it has been my privilege to work beside at Celtic Park over the years.

For all the money that Rangers have spent, and regard-less of who they've brought to Ibrox, I don't believe there is

Each of these supporters paid for the privilege of playing at Celtic Park before my testimonial game. I'm lucky, I get on to the park for nothing!

one as gifted as Paul McStay. To my way of thinking, Paul is unquestionably the best player in Scotland. If he had decided to go to the continent, Paul could have earned himself untold fortunes by this time, but he is obviously another one for whom there are things in life that are more important than money. Paul McStay doesn't have an agent and brought his father along with him when he discussed his last contract with Celtic. The entire McStay family is as steeped in the club as it is possible to be, and the three sons who have all played for the team, Willie and Raymond as well as Paul, are a credit to their mother and father as human beings and not just as footballers. Roy Aitken is another who, by his inclination to play for Celtic and no other club, is worthy of the gratitude of everyone associated with Celtic.

Personally speaking, I have always wanted Celtic to mean as much to other people as they have meant to me and to ask that everyone gives the maximum effort for the team. I would freely admit that I have, in the past, allowed that sense of conviction to overheat and let my temper get the better of me to an embarrassing degree.

When I was a teenager on the groundstaff, I once had a row with another player that became so animated I ended up with a broken nose. It took place behind one of the goals at Celtic Park during a training session when I had a spectacular difference of opinion with a youngster called Bernie Little. One word very quickly led to another and the next thing I knew we were scrapping on the ground. A third party, Mick Kelly, tried to intervene but as a peace-maker he wasn't in the Henry Kissinger class, and in the general mêlée his hand caught my nose and put it, quite literally, out of joint. Once we had all calmed down, a story had to be invented for the benefit of Bob Rooney, who was then Celtic's trainer, to the effect that I had accidentally run into a goal-post.

This wild streak of mine is something I have never been able to curb and I can still have my moments in training, as team-mates past and present will be able to testify. All I can say is that I am always overcome by regrets afterwards and full of apologies. The story of my broken nose is only of value as an example of my obsession with Celtic and because it enables me to introduce the argument that affection for any club on that scale may no longer exist in the future as loyalty gradually diminishes until it finally becomes a thing of the past.

I know that Celtic supporters respect the players at our club to the extent that they think of them as the chosen few who are not actually ordinary mortals with gas bills to pay and shoes to buy for the children. In the years ahead it is going to be increasingly difficult for Celtic and everybody else, however, to stop the market place becoming freer by the minute, and that will not be for the want of trying on the part of club managements as they attempt to retain the strongest possible squad of players.

Obviously it's different for me now because I've arrived at that stage in my career where I'm contented in every way. I have worked out in my own mind the playing contri-

Laughing with a legend. Kenny Dalglish, the greatest Scottish footballer of all time and myself before my Testimonial match against Liverpool in 1987.

bution that I have made to Celtic since the mid-seventies and there are no feelings of frustration over what might have been when I reflect on the past as I have experienced it at club or international level. There was a period when my fixation with Celtic got so bad that Davie Hay, during his time as manager, had to take me to the one side and tell me that I couldn't go on taking my work home with me, and his advice was greatly appreciated. Basically, I stopped going about worrying over whether I was living up to other people's expectations of what I should have been achieving and learned to be my own best judge. Other people are great at inventing ambitions for you, which was another thing I worked out for myself. I learned to solve all my problems by talking to myself in the car going home and ending the self-analysis before I got to the front door

E

and became a husband and father to Rosemary and the children.

I like to think I've always been a good listener, receptive to ideas and instructions, since I was taught at the feet of Jock Stein, Willie Fernie and people like that. I also feel I'm looking into a mirror when I watch our assistant manager, Tommy Craig, working with the players at Celtic Park. He is another who is dedicated to Celtic and wants everyone about him to share that depth of feeling. The arch motivator, though, has to be Billy McNeill. I have been responding to his passion for the club for a long time but he is still the person who can get me motivated like no other for any game. These are the people who are the living embodiment of Celtic's spirit and they enjoy the absolute respect of the supporters for that reason.

It is important to know you have that unreserved support, and I got confirmation of my entry into the select band on the Sunday afternoon in August, 1987 when Celtic played Liverpool in my testimonial match. That occasion will stand forever as my greatest moment as a Celtic player. I can recall every moment of the day as clearly now as when it happened. I arrived at the ground at half past twelve as a bag of nerves and was unable to unwind. Because of the nature of these occasions, I was the only one playing who was not allowed to come out of the dressing-room and loosen up on the pitch, since I was being held back for a grand entrance. The waiting was definitely the worst part because it gave me time to think about how big, or how small, the crowd would be by the time I did get outside for a look at the terracings. I wouldn't like anyone to get the impression that I was sitting there coldly calculating how much I would earn out of the day per thousand people or anything like that. For me, a small turn-out would have meant that I had failed as a Celtic player, regardless of how many medals I had in the display cabinet, with every blank space in the ground a painful reminder of that fact.

Being a success at Celtic Park is measured in more ways

I was one of the boys from the 'Jungle' who was lucky enough to wear the jersey. After the Liverpool game, I gave the jersey back to the people.

than one. Playing a part in the winning of trophies is one thing, but establishing a special rapport with the supporters was equally important to me. When the moment came for the rest of the side to go out without me, I was left completely alone in the dressing room for fully five minutes, which can seem like an eternity under those circumstances. It did leave me time, though, to sit there and take a lingering look at the place while the memories flooded back. I thought of that first, awkward conversation with Jock Stein while I was on the groundstaff and how I used to gather up the towels for Billy McNeill, Jimmy Johnstone and Bobby Lennox when I was still 'wee Tommy' from the Calton.

My solitude was interrupted when there came a knock at the door and Tony McGuiness, a West of Scotland businessman who was a member of my testimonial committee, asked me if I was ready. I was actually on my knees in the shower room at the time offering up a quiet prayer of thanks for the long professional life I had been given at Celtic Park. When I came down the tunnel and saw the sea of hands raised upwards in acclamation it was an emotionally humbling moment. I ran instinctively to that part of the ground known as the 'jungle' because that houses the most fervently committed of the team's supporters. My natural inclination at that stage was to scale the fencing in front of the crowd and jump in beside them because I was beginning to feel totally overwhelmed. A testimonial is something that is discussed by the club well in advance of its taking place, and yet when the moment arrives it is hard for the person being honoured to take it all in and absorb all the affection that is shown to him. I have a video recording of my big day at home and I still look at it from time to time while never failing to feel the hairs on the back of my head standing on end. Occasions like that will, in all probability, become obsolete unless players are kept on a sufficiently high pay scale to keep them at one club and make the prospect of exercising freedom of contract the less attractive option, which is a pity.

Speaking purely as an individual who would like to see Celtic prosper and grow in this new world that is coming along, if the club were to offer ways of letting the supporters invest in the team, providing the money to entice and hold players, I would be the first in what I'm sure would be a lengthy queue. Whatever scheme the club care to come up with, the people will go for it and I still think, as they do, that the improvement of the team gets priority over renovating the ground.

If there was a willingness to turn over 49% of the club's total shareholding to the general public, leaving the controlling majority in the hands of the board, they would be bought out of sentimentality but also with a proper appreciation of helping create a sound financial base from which to work. In some ways it's sad that the game is gradually losing its soul to commercialism, and it would be hard to say that any of what is happening off the park is for the better. Does the ordinary Rangers supporter, for instance, feel he has started to lose touch with his club the more grandiose their plans have become to create an executive class of spectator? If all clubs bring in properly trained personnel with a background in business studies and try to emulate what Rangers have done, though, who knows where the game might end up in Scotland?

It could even be that Rangers themselves will feel secure enough in their own, inordinately wealthy position to sign more than one Catholic to play for them. For all that they have done to restore and revitalise the whole of the Scottish League, the one blemish on their record was a signing policy, which, prior to Mo Johnston, looked primitive beside everything else. It is not as if breaking down that last, provocative barrier need be thought of as being so huge a step it will alter the social fabric of the entire country, because Rangers, like Celtic, will always be thought of in the same way so far as background is concerned. Besides which, they have had a Jewish player, Avi Cohen, who was actually excused from playing during the holy time of Yom Kippur by Graeme Souness. Rangers also have a coloured personality in Mark Walters, and it is my belief that he is the best of all the Englishmen at Ibrox because he has a unique playing style and is an entertainer who is certainly capable of reminding us that the game can be beautiful to look at.

When Mark was the target for mindless, racist abuse, I was as disgusted as any right-thinking person of any race, creed or colour would have been. In that instance I would like to think Rangers considered the feelings of a group of people who were discriminated against on the grounds of religious persuasion for a long number of years. Signing a Catholic, Mo Johnston, for Ibrox will not wipe out bigotry at a stroke but it will take away the notion that, even in these most sophisticated times for that club, Rangers will tolerate in their colours players of any persuasion. And the game is getting hard enough to handle without any unnecessary difficulties being thrown in.

CHAPTER NINE

The Other Side of Me

In November, 1988 at the twilight of Celtic's centenary year but when it was still possible to recall with absolute clarity the winning of the Premier League Championship and the Scottish Cup a few months before, Billy McNeill called me into his office and asked me how I felt about taking over the manager's job with Partick Thistle. In the immortal words of Michael Caine, whether or not he ever used them, not a lot of people know that. What Billy didn't tell me, either, as he raised the subject was that he had formally turned down the proposal before I walked into his room. I was simply informed that a member of the Partick Thistle board of directors had asked Celtic if I was available to take over and had requested my reaction to the idea.

I can truthfully say now that temptation never crossed my mind and I explained to the manager that this was because it was still my deepest wish to continue playing for Celtic for as long as I possibly could and that I felt I was also capable of contributing towards the winning of even more trophies. It was only then that Billy told me there was no chance of Celtic agreeing to release me from my contract, in any case. I was then 31 years old and I imagined that Celtic felt that, if I was moving on, they could have sold me to another club rather than give me away to someone who was going to get a player for nothing as well as filling a managerial vacancy at the same time. If Billy was testing the depth of my commitment to Celtic while he was at it, then he was entitled to take stock of someone who had been on the staff for fourteen years, but I can only say now what I said then and that is that I will know when the time is right to go.

My answer had nothing at all to do with not wanting to join Partick Thistle, either, because I wouldn't look down my nose at any club who showed an interest in me and I would like to add that I think they got a very good man for the job in John Lambie. The idea of player/management is a comparatively new one in this country, anyway, and has also shown itself to be full of pitfalls. How can a man, in his guise of club boss, for example, refuse to listen to any player's wage demands during contractual negotiations and then go out on to the park with him later on the same week and expect that individual to give his all for the team? Also, how can the manager criticise on the park and hope to get the correct response when he may not be playing well enough to justify picking himself?

When the time comes for me to contemplate moving into management — and I hope it is still some way off yet — I will have done all I possibly can in the playing sense at Celtic Park and will be interested only in putting back into the game what I think is relevant and will help bring back some of the beauty of football for the paying public. Whenever Celtic had no game, I used to go through the turnstiles and stand on the terracing at various grounds but I gave up the practice a few years ago because it wasn't worth the money, the time or the effort. I have my own philosophy on the game and how it should be played and I will be looking for a chance to put those ideas into operation. By then, I would like to think that clubs will have moved closer to the continental way of working, whereby the person in my position would be in charge of team matters and nothing else because that can be a complex enough job on its own. It stands to reason that the more administrative burdens are removed from the manager's shoulders, the better he will be able to concentrate on what he is actually paid to do.

As the reader will have appreciated by now, this book is not, and was never intended to be, about sharing dressing-room gossip or tales outside my club or anybody else's. I don't particularly care about which players did what while

In the thick of it against Partick Thistle, who could have had me as their manager a few months later.

they were on tour or playing in European competition. Call me a killjoy or anything else you like but I have always believed that the game was too serious, and affected the lives of too many people, to be unnecessarily flippant about it. I feel that way about Celtic because that is how I was brought up to think about the club but I would be the same wherever I was if I had a side of my own to look after because football affects me deeply.

I have never played golf, for instance, which makes me out of the ordinary among my fellow professionals, or indulged in any recreational activity during all the years I have been with Celtic. Apart from listening to music at home and giving a fairly spirited rendition of 'Mack the Knife' when the occasion merits my impersonation of

Bobby Darin, I have nothing that occupies my mind, or excites me, the way the game of football does. If that sounds like boyish naivety then I am not ashamed to be called one, the other or both. The next generation of players coming along are mercenaries, interested only in how much money they will get for playing rather than who they will play for and how they will lend themselves to the team once they get on to the park. Our game and American football will soon seem not that far apart in terms of tactical approach because it will be about one side totally nullifying the other and it will be up to a new breed of managers to see if they can reverse this distressing trend wherever possible.

When the time comes for me to go into management, I will, temperamentally, come into the category of what I would call the lunatic variety. One day, I will be in a dressing room at half-time throwing about the cups and saucers in the time-honoured fashion of the more melodramatic members of the profession. The most successful in that line, like Jim McLean, Alex Ferguson, Graeme Souness and Billy McNeill, are hardly placid by nature and when it comes to getting across what they want from players on match days, that's the forceful approach required. I have attended the S.F.A.'s coaching course in Largs and one of the main prerequisites needed for getting your final certificate is the ability to hold the attention of the group of players you're working with and imparting your message quickly and concisely. Man management is also about knowing how to handle the different temperaments that will make up the team in your dressing room.

Football has made me do things that would sound like strange behaviour to the average person in the street. In the days that lead up to a big game in whatever competition, my stomach muscles feel as if they're permanently knotted together and that sensation will only go once the referee blows his whistle and the match begins. It would not be the first time, either, that I have found my sleep afterwards reduced to a couple of hours when that game is

O.K. for me . . . O.K. for me and Mark McGhee.

over, and that is whether Celtic have won, lost or drawn. Under those circumstances, all I can do is get up, go downstairs and sit in the darkness of my own living room with a bottle of milk in my hand going over and over the course of play in my mind once again. There was a time in my life when I felt so tense as a result of the constant pressure that I used to say to myself, 'I'll be glad when all of this is over and I can retire.'

I no longer think of things that way, though, because, for better or worse, this is what I do best in life and, as I have said about players lending themselves to the game, I think the individual has to lend himself to the game of life as well. There would be no point in me going out of the game and then spending my time as a cantankerous ex-professional telling everyone in sight how this manager or that one has made a mistake and how I would have handled it all so much better. I now know I want to immerse myself in that side of the game, make my own mistakes and find out for myself if I'm suited to the job. If I was to fail, it wouldn't be the end of the world, either. We are all insignificant little dots on the face of the earth and it would be wrong to get carried away by my own self-importance in relation to a humble game of football. Not being a successful manager would hardly make me, or anybody else, any less of a human being, would it?

When the time comes, of course, there will be occasions when I will forget all of those sensible words and become absorbed to the point of irrationality. Players, though, will put up with a manager ranting and raving if they understand that, basically, he knows what he's talking about where the game is concerned. The first thing any player can detect is a counterfeit coach who doesn't have the tactical know-how. I am confident enough in my own capabilities to believe that I will progress and I already have in mind the names of the men I would like to work with me wherever I am destined to go after Celtic Park. Whoever they are, I will still end up in the darkened room in the middle of the night, but, to be honest, I have tried marinating my moods in alcohol and I would have to say that, on the whole, I would rather remember in the morning what had kept me up in the first place.

Devotion to football was once summed up by saying that it was the ordinary supporter entrusting his happiness to eleven men for an hour and a half without having any control over how they treated his emotional commitment. Club management will be even worse for me when the time comes because I will be placing my job security in the hands of a group of players I will personally be unable to help once the most important shift of the week begins. To those who are not wrapped up in the game, all of this must make those of us who are professionally involved, or are impassioned spectators, a type of people beyond understanding and who have an unnatural attachment to something we are guilty of making sound more important than it really is.

I would try to put the argument into perspective by

referring back to the game Celtic played against Liverpool in aid of the ninety-five people who died and the families bereaved by the disaster at Sheffield Wednesday's Hillsborough stadium. If ever an incident strongly reinforced the realisation that football is about twenty-two men chasing after a piece of air-filled white leather, it was that day in April, 1989 when Liverpool were playing Nottingham Forest in the semi finals of the F.A. Cup. Two weeks later, after the last burial had taken place, Celtic staged a match to raise funds for the dependents and when I walked out to look at the ground on the morning of the match the sight that greeted me made the hairs on the back of my neck stand on end. A line of Liverpool supporters' banners stretched from one end of our terracing to the other, but not in a way that gave me an eerie feeling. Football clubs in cities like Liverpool or Glasgow are thought of as institutions by those who support them and it is important to the people concerned that this commitment to the cause is handed down from one generation to another.

Football in that environment is about myths, fables and mass emotion that can become like a communicable disease. That is why it was fundamentally correct that, after a respectful period of mourning had been observed, Liverpool resumed playing their remaining games that season. It was what their people, even those who had been personally affected by the tragedy, wanted and it is a fact that life must go on. I saw the faces of the Liverpool players on the day of our match with them and I realised I was looking at close range into the eyes of men who had observed closely the unspeakable grief of others in a way that had left them deeply moved.

Having said all that, I am a footballer and not a sociologist, but I also know that when the players of both teams and their wives went to a reception given later by Glasgow District Council, the feeling of relief hung heavily in the air over Kenny Dalglish and those who had walked in behind him. Everyone associated with Liverpool conducted themselves with great dignity throughout that terrible time, and nobody more so than Kenny himself, but the act of putting their boots on once again was the start of the healing process. What had gone before was not about martyrdom, though, but the ability of a football club to embrace people's emotions and expectations.

There are limits I would not exceed in order to pursue a career in management, however, and sacrificing my family life would be one of them. This is not to say I do not have the utmost sympathy for, and understanding of, the position in which Rangers' manager, Graeme Souness, found himself when he remained in Scotland while his wife and children went abroad.

I accept that the post of Rangers manager has, since the takeover of the club that followed Graeme's arrival from Italy in 1986, come with a different set of rules from those used by the rest of us. It seems as if clubs who are as big even as Celtic still have their feet on the ground in their everyday dealings and are, therefore, still of this world. Rangers, on the other hand, have gone through the roof in their business dealings on and off the park and are heading for a planet of their own. It isn't easy, either, trying to operate within the fishbowl of the city of Glasgow, where stories about players and managers are the currency of conversation in any social setting or place of work.

It isn't difficult to become the talk of the steamie and I have had my moments. As I said earlier, I know I will have a hair-trigger temper to match any of the present crop of managers. It is unavoidable because as any of my team-mates, past or present, will readily testify, I have fought with more people than anyone at Celtic Park. There have been violent, physical arguments with Johnny Doyle, Davie Provan, Frank McGarvey, Dominic Sullivan and countless others. I will own up to any of that, but where I must put the record straight is over the pub talk that I once had to be suspended by Celtic for a period of ten days because I had a fist fight with Roy Aitken after a Celtic-Rangers match. The date of the game was April Fool's

Scoring against the hoops; but the blue and white variety of Kilmarnock.

Day, 1989 and I have often wondered if that was totally apt for this particular piece of fiction built around a game which we lost and which helped Rangers move nearer to the championship. Because both Roy and myself were immediately removed from the squad of players who flew out to Dubai later that weekend for a friendly match against Liverpool, the rumour factory went into full production.

If I had raised my hands in the dressing room because I blamed Roy for not taking the penalty that we missed and cost ourselves at least one point, I would be the first to admit it. After all, it has never required the particularly intense pressure of an Old Firm match to get me worked up. Earlier that same season, for instance, Mick McCarthy and myself had to be pulled apart in the dressing room and that was after we had eliminated a First Division side, Clydebank, from the Scottish Cup on our own ground. Mick is the type of person who could find it in himself to shake hands with me before we left Celtic Park that night and players accept that this kind of thing goes on under stress. In fact, Mick made a point of saying he would miss the passion of Scottish football when he left Celtic for Olympique Lyons.

If I get a club of my own to run, I will also be able to carry that level of understanding over with me from the dressing room to the manager's office. Players who become managers are like poachers turned gamekeepers, but it all depends to what degree you allow that to happen. So long as the man in charge continues to remember what it was like for him as a player, he can understand the root causes of any team problems. Essentially, players want to take, take, take out of the game, and it is what the manager can make them give while fighting for the best deal on their behalf that is important. Obviously, discipline has to be maintained but an appreciation of what players are going through is vital. I wouldn't want to be someone who would tell his team how it was in my day but rather get commitment by putting myself in their position at any given time and earning their respect.

For me, good management is about being a good actor ninety per cent of the time. One other characteristic that players have is the total lack of any objection to having their ego's massaged at regular intervals. When I was younger I was capable of listening to praise from certain quarters and wandering away thinking that I was some player.

Later on, though, I learned to heed only what was said to me by my closest friends outside Celtic Park, like the people I was brought up with in the Calton. Gerry Collins, who is a professional player, and John Jarvis, who isn't but is a good judge of the game, are totally honest in their assessment of anything I do. However, if it takes the psychology of man management to get the best out of the players I'll be working with, then I will use all the kidology necessary.

What I need when the time comes is a strong personality

in charge of a club somewhere to give me a chance to put theory into practice. I never want to be judged on my suitability for any job, and then discarded, because I was, and still am, a Celtic man. By the same token, I don't want to be given a position solely for that reason, either. I want to be encouraged by a man who knows that I can give his club what they need. Football is the one thing I know something about and it wouldn't have to be a club with all the facilities I have enjoyed at Celtic Park to get me interested and excited. I'm looking for stimulation, not surroundings. Even if it meant a part-time club and a budget that didn't allow for spending money on the best of players, it would be satisfying getting the maximum effort out of the staff who were there in the first place. It is any player's capacity for learning that is important. If the individual has ability, that talent can be channelled for the good of the team. Nobody was born to play in just one position, in my opinion. If you can play football and take in what you're being taught, you can play anywhere. The hardest change of position for me, I suppose, will be leaving the only club I ever wanted to play for and making my way in the game somewhere else. But not only is it inevitable that I will have to make that move from Celtic Park; it is probably essential I do so for a variety of reasons.

CHAPTER TEN

Seeking Managerial Asylum

Fate, like Tommy Burns, twists and turns, and football is not the kind of profession in which anything can be relied upon. My first priority after my playing career is over will be to establish myself not only as a respected coach but as the very best in the business, wherever I go. In order to do that, I will one day have to sever my working relationship with Celtic. How, though, do you walk away from the one thing that has, apart from your family, meant most in life to you? The answer is with a great deal of difficulty but also an appreciation that Celtic can not teach me what I need to know about handling players.

First of all, Celtic already have a clearly defined management structure, with Billy McNeill and Tommy Craig looking after the first team and Benny Rooney and Bobby Lennox in charge of the reserve side and development of the youth players. Bearing in mind, too, that it's only manners to be asked if you're wanted in the first place, I need job experience at the sharp end of the business and not a position that has been created out of gratitude to a former servant. There is an argument that it is not possible to learn any more from a small club than can be picked up at the highest level of the game inside a place like Celtic Park. I think you have to come out from underneath the protection of others, be your own man and progress, or fail, by making your own mistakes.

I need to find out for myself what makes individual players tick and how to be ruthless, if necessary, with them. Being uncompromising will not be difficult because a lengthy career in the game makes you that way and I know now that I am ready to stand up on my own. As recently as my mid-twenties, when the thought of Arsenal wanting to sign me threw me into a panic, that was not the case, but I have endured a lot in my life since then and I am a different person.

I surely have no need, either, to go on record as stating that I hope Billy stays in the job for as long as he is happy to lead Celtic. I have learned a lot from him about the psychological side of the business and often had it drawn to my attention that there is always something new to think about. Would it surprise anyone to know, for instance, that on the night before Celtic beat Rangers in the Scottish Cup final on May 20, 1989 the manager actively encouraged his players to have a two-hour-long party at our hotel in Seamill? It is perfectly true that Celtic go there before big matches basically to eat, sleep and train and do very little else. On that occasion, though, there were forces at work which made it essential to release the safety valve that was containing the pressure building up before a game which was crucial to our reputation.

Among the many ways in which Celtic are different from any other club is the fierce pride we have in our record as the greatest Cup-fighting side of them all. We have won the Scottish Cup more times than anyone else and when we were publicly written off before facing Rangers, of all people, it had the effect of creating a formidable team spirit.

On the eve of the game it was reckoned that we were inferior to our oldest rivals and were coming to the end of a season in which we had won nothing and had never looked like winning anything either. The job that Billy McNeill did in bringing our motivation to the boil at the right time was magnificent. There was a club trip to Portugal the week before the final, during which the team blew away their previous cares and woes with a day of golf, followed by a memorable night out and then two days of hard work on the specific tactics that won us the final by the only goal of the game. It was at Seamill, though, that Billy showed he was a master at handling players sensitively at vital moments.

Our meals are served to us as a team group in a special room at the hotel, which was just as well in this instance because the party atmosphere broke out with a vengeance before the plates were cleared away. Aerosol sprays containing string and foam were produced and when I say everybody in the official party responded to the idea of letting off steam, I mean everybody. Even our masseur, Jimmy Steele, who is in his seventies, put on a grotesque mask and entered into the spirit of the occasion. We were offending no-one by our behaviour and it wasn't a case of big-headed footballers doing as they liked and then walking off to leave others to clean up their mess behind them. Before going off to bed, twenty revellers put in five pounds each so that the cleaning staff would be well looked after for dealing with the debris from what you could have called a group therapy session.

By the time the players put one foot out the side of their beds on the day of the final, our first thought was, 'Right, let's go and get a result at Hampden.' Once again, Billy McNeill had wound us up like an alarm clock that went off when he pressed the button. The party trick had first been done to create a mood at the semi-final stage, when people were beginning to wonder if Hibs were catching us at a vulnerable moment.

Billy McNeill is also a superstitious man and what had worked the night before the semi final had to be done again a month later. It was what happened after Joe Miller scored Celtic's winning goal that day which makes it so hard for someone like me to contemplate the moment I will have to say 'goodbye', be it temporarily or for good, to the club on a professional basis. In between the official, Cup-winning reception, which was held at Celtic Park, and the impromptu celebrations, which took place in Mark McGhee's house, Pat Bonner, myself and our two wives, Ann and Rosemary, did what thousands of others did and went to the pub. The only difference was that we got paid

£1,000 for charity for having our drink. There is a bar that is well known to Celtic supporters, called Heraghty's, on the South side of Glasgow. Pat and myself had been promised that, in the event of Celtic winning the Cup, we would get that money for a children's charity if we went in there and sang 'When Irish Eyes Are Smiling'. The pair of us went in and proved that as well as it being a grand old team to play for it is also a 'grand' old team to sing for!

Heraghty's is like a magnet to Celtic supporters from all walks of life and I find our following to be broadly based, if equally fanatical. I am honoured every year by the students of the combined Edinburgh University and Heriot Watt University Celtic Supporters Club when they have their 'Tommy Burns Supper'. There are no poetry recitals, only Celtic songs instead, and the immortal memory is of the club's past deeds. Whoever, wherever our supporters are, they have long honoured me and yet, on the night of the Cup Final, I knew that they might have revised their opinions of me had the result gone the other way against Rangers. Then it would have been the case that Burns was too old, past it and no longer had the legs to carry him through a hectic season.

I went home from Mark McGhee's house as sober as a judge so that I could remember every detail of the game and its aftermath and lay awake all night considering my performance and the consequences of the result against Rangers. I consider my contribution to have been one of the most disciplined day's work I have ever done for Celtic and it helped convince me that so long as I have younger, sturdier legs about me, I can play for Billy McNeill in a worthwhile way until well into the 1990s. I think my delight after the game was over at Hampden, when I spent so long cavorting about the Celtic end of the ground that I almost missed the presentation of the medals, summed up the importance of that day for me.

Of course it wasn't just the fact that Celtic had saved themselves from a season without a major trophy that wa important; the idea that we had prevented Rangers fro winning the treble at the same time also had a definite appeal. For lots of Celtic supporters, beating Rangers is the single most important part of any season and the feeling is entirely mutual, I'm sure. Since so many English-born players started to arrive at Ibrox under Graeme Souness, I have wondered if they are as aware of the old rivalries as their own supporters would like them to be. The reason for being able even to pose that question was the game in which Celtic lost 5-1 to Rangers in August, 1988. The only thing going through my mind that afternoon was the imminent danger of a certain 7-1 scoreline that has been daubed on the walls of Glasgow's buildings for posterity having to be removed and replaced by something more embarrassing in a different colour. Was it the case, though, that the majority of Rangers' players did not know their followers had been taunted since 1957 by the reminder of Celtic's win in the League Cup final?

At 5-1 in Rangers' favour, and with twenty minutes still left to play at Ibrox, Graeme Souness' players certainly had the opportunity to rewrite history and create a milestone of their own that would have taken decades to live down, if it ever could have been wiped out, but they seemed content to rest on what they had achieved. That sums up the basic difference between the native-born and those bought in. Scots on either side of the Old Firm divide are brought up with the statistics, the songs and the realisation of how seriously it is all taken by the people on the terracing.

I appeared on television the day after that still horrific result at Ibrox, and for one reason only. Dignity in defeat like that can have its own value and I think I made my point as honestly as I could when I said I was only glad Rangers hadn't scored seven or more. There are many negative aspects of the Old Firm rivalry but I believe that the clubs are good for each other. If neither Celtic nor Rangers are doing particularly well, as when Aberdeen and Dundee United won enough honours to merit being called the New Firm in the early eighties, the supporters in the West can handle it because there is no imbalance in their eyes. If one half of Glasgow looks like becoming the dominant force, however, the other is compelled to do something about it, mainly by way of buying new players.

Having said that, I would nominate as the four most talented players associated with Celtic during my time with the club a quartet who cost nothing because they were brought through the scouting system. I could have filled these pages with stories of wayward individuals who became involved with drink and women before matches, but who's interested in that kind of stuff? Players who have been a credit to the game and themselves as well as giving pleasure to spectators of all ages surely deserve to have their ability recognised before the tawdrier 'talents' possessed by others I could mention.

The finest contemporary player ever to come out of Scotland is Kenny Dalglish. I can't say too much about him in a Celtic context because he had gone from the club to Liverpool before I had properly established myself in the first team, but Kenny would be able to lay claim to the title of Scotland's greatest player of all time. The best Celtic player in my time as a regular member of the side has been Paul McStay. I have heard it said that Paul can be held back on the park by his own personality and that if he had a more arrogant streak he would be an even better player. To my way of thinking, that is absolute rubbish. Arrogance leads to carelessness and bad habits, both on and off the park. Any player should always be trying for maximum efficiency and that is what Paul McStay does. He is also not so big a star he can't take a telling from time to time, either. If you can show Paul the error of his ways in the dressing room, he will accept that criticism without believing that he is above reproach.

It has always been a source of amazement and frustration to me that so many top, international class players can go through their careers without absorbing too many lessons.

I am not saying that, as a manager, I would ever attempt

to stifle any kind of spontaneity but I would try to increase the awareness of whoever was in my team.

The most naturally gifted player I ever worked beside was Charlie Nicholas. The only pity was that Charlie didn't stay long enough with Celtic to be able to be considered for selection as one of the club's all-time greats. That kind of accolade can only be bestowed after a lengthy track record of having done it year in, year out for Celtic has been established. That is why the player I admired most at Celtic Park was Danny McGrain. Adversity can have the effect of lifting people to fresh heights of effort and application and that was certainly the case with Danny, who survived a fractured skull early in his career, followed by diabetes and then a mysterious ankle ailment that cost him a year out of his playing life. I have always put my faith in God to help get me through any crisis that I find too hard to bear on my own. Danny fought back on his own, with the most incredibly single-minded attitude I have ever seen at work and also a sense of humour that never failed him in spite of all he had been through.

Danny was also involved in what I will think back on as the two most courageous and fulfilling displays of my time with Celtic. When we defeated Sporting Lisbon in the U.E.F.A. Cup by five clear goals at Celtic Park it was the most exhilarating combination of team spirit on the park and inspirational backing off it that I can ever recall. We were two goals behind from the first leg and although Celtic do not go out deliberately to make life difficult for ourselves there is no doubt that, once upset, we react to drawbacks in a way that has more than earned us our reputation as a side with a flair for the dramatic.

The team who won the League Championship in 1986 by beating St. Mirren at Love Street, also by five clear goals, was probably not good enough to win the title but nobody bothered about that inside the dressing room. All we knew was that Celtic were being written off and that the experts had as good as installed Hearts as Champions.

We kept on going until we proved the pundits wrong,

and to provide the inspiration behind an achievement like that would give any manager immense cause for satisfaction. That is why I have to find out if I am capable of doing something like that for myself. That would mean devoting myself to the players out in the fresh air and not being desk-bound. It is necessary to know, administratively speaking, what is going on inside your club but any manager's first priority should be to see that enough time is being spent where it really matters. There should never be any danger that players are suffering through lack of attention on the manager's part.

I have disciplined myself throughout my professional career and made sacrifices where my private life was concerned. It will be the same when I move into the next phase of my working life. Football has given me a means of earning a living that would have been denied me had I left St. Mary's Secondary School without an educational certificate or the offer of a job with Celtic. The game has helped make me a better person, too, because of the good habits I have had to develop in order to keep myself playing at the highest level for so many years. If it hadn't been for Celtic, I would have been wandering about the Calton with no particular notion of what I was going to do next. I'm not saying I would have turned into a villain to get the things I wanted because the fact of the matter is I never had the nerve to contemplate a life of crime. I was always too afraid of the police to stray from the straight and narrow, and it was just as well the wee boy from the hard background was being looked after by the man above.

My own children wouldn't last ten minutes in the Calton because that environment is not what they're used to, but I am grateful that I have been able to provide them with a lifestyle that has been good for them. They will undoubtedly learn to make their own way in the world and if my son, Michael, wants to pursue a career in football when he is old enough I will certainly not raise any objections. How could I? While there were some people I was brought up with who, through no fault of their own, had lives without direction or sense of purpose, football laid out a path in front of me. It was my extreme good fortune that this path led down Soho Street to London Road and stretched the few hundred yards from there to the front door at 95 Kerrydale Street, the home of Celtic. I was the supporter who was lucky enough to get the hooped jersey to wear and become the people's representative on the park.

It is touching to know you have had an effect on the lives of folk you have never met, and the emotional bond with the supporters has been an integral part of the enjoyment I have had since 1975. This, though, is only the last chapter of my book and not the end of the story. I still have ambitions on my own behalf at Celtic Park and I'm not just trying to put off the day that will inevitably dawn when I must go from the club. It will, I freely admit, be very hard to walk out that door for the last time as a player but, when that moment comes, I will know exactly the size of the contribution I have made to Celtic. I have got the medals to measure my place in the club's history and no-one will ever be able to take them, and the memories they inspire, from me. Thank God.

International Caps

1981				
May	v	Northern Ireland	(h)	2·0
1982				
March	v	Holland	(h)	2·1
May	v	Wales	(h)	1·0
December	v	Belgium	(a)	2·3
1983				
May	v	Northern Ireland	(h)	0·0
June	v	Canada	(Toronto)	2·0
June	v	Canada	(Vancouver)	2·0
1988				
May	v	England	(a)	0·1

Appearances and Goals for Celtic

	LEAGUE	LEAGUE CUP	SCOTTISH CUP	EUROPE	GOALS
1974-75	1 (s)	—	—	—	—
1975-76	5	—	—	—	—
1976-77	13 + 9(s)	6	1 + 2(s)	1	1
1977-78	22 + 2(s)	6	3	3	6
1978-79	28 + 1(s)	8	3	4	5
1979-80	12 + 3(s)	—	1 + 1(s)	2 + 1(s)	1
1980-81	32 + 1(s)	7	5	3	11
1981-82	33	6	2	2	9
1982-83	17	8	1	1	10
1983-84	33 + 1(s)	11	5	6	13
1984-85	25 + 2(s)	3	4 + 2(s)	4	10

	LEAGUE	LEAGUE CUP	SCOTTISH CUP	EUROPE	GOALS
1985-86	34	3	3	2	6
1986-87	14 + 3(s)	3	—	3	—
1987-88	21 + 6(s)	3	5	2	4
1988-89	30 + 1(s)	3	5	3	7

Index